SPANISH NEW MEXICO

SPANISH NEW MEXICO

Edited by DONNA PIERCE and MARTA WEIGLE
With a Foreword by Anita Gonzales Thomas
Photographs by Jack Parsons
Concept and Design by William Field

VOLUME TWO: HISPANIC ARTS IN THE TWENTIETH CENTURY

MUSEUM OF NEW MEXICO PRESS
SANTA FE

THE SPANISH COLONIAL ARTS SOCIETY COLLECTION

CONTENTS

VOLUME ONE: THE ARTS OF SPANISH NEW MEXICO

CONTENTS

VOLUME TWO: HISPANIC ARTS IN THE TWENTIETH CENTURY

Project Editor: Mary Wachs
Manuscript Editor: Jenifer Blakemore
Concept and Design: William Field
Composition: Mindy Holmes, Copygraphics
Manufactured in Korea by Sung In Printing
10 9 8 7 6 5 4 3 2 1

Library of Congress Cataloging–in–Publication Data
Spanish Colonial Arts Society.
    Spanish New Mexico : the Spanish Colonial Arts Society collection /
edited by Donna Pierce and Marta Weigle ; photographs by Jack Parsons.
        p. cm.
    Contents: v. 1. The arts of Spanish New Mexico — v. 2. Hispanic arts in the
twentieth century.
    ISBN 0-89013-311-5 (2 vol. slipcased). — ISBN 0-89013-309-3 (vol. 1 :
pbk.). — ISBN 0-89013-310-7 (vol. 2 : pbk.)
    1. Decorative arts, Spanish colonial—New Mexico—Catalogs. 2. Hispanic
decorative arts—New Mexico—Catalogs. 3. Decorative arts—New Mexico—
Santa Fe—Catalogs. 4. Spanish Colonial Arts Society—Catalogs. I. Pierce,
Donna, 1950-   . II. Weigle, Marta III. Title.
    NK835.N5S62   1996
    745'.09789'07478956—dc20   96-16130
                                                                CIP

MUSEUM OF NEW MEXICO PRESS
Post Office Box 2087
Santa Fe, New Mexico 87504

FOREWORD

When the Spanish explorer Don Juan de Oñate arrived in New Mexico in 1598, he was accompanied by hundreds of Spanish families who dreamed of making the New World their new home. As they slowly settled into their strange new environment they hung on to those parts of their own culture that they would need to survive. Foremost among these was their belief in God, a belief that was part of their very being. As Paul Horgan wrote in his 1954 classic, *Great River: The Rio Grande in North American History,* "It was a divine company they kept. . . . The Holy Family and the saints inhabited their soul, thoughts and words."

Fortified by their religious beliefs and their close family ties, the early settlers endured many dangers and hardships. They created a satisfying pastoral and agricultural life attuned to the rhythm of the seasons and the liturgical year of the church. They loved this beautiful, harsh land and clung tenaciously to their cherished cultural traditions. Through family and faith both they and their traditions endured. I grew up in Santa Fe, New Mexico, early in this century as part of that same Spanish culture that was transplanted here so many years ago. Now, as I observe this culture moving toward the end of the century, I am proud to say

ANITA GONZALES THOMAS

that the importance of family and faith still survives. Many of the customs that the early settlers brought to the region are still practiced by Hispanic families in New Mexico each day. And although times have changed the cultural significance of these ancient customs has not. In those old times, the day began at dawn with the singing of the *alba,* a hymn of thanksgiving and praise, with all the household joining in. Those of us who like to get up early still begin our day with the ancient prayer, *Bendita sea la luz y la santa vera cruz,* "Blessed be the light and the holy true cross." I was thrilled several years ago, upon reading Samuel Eliot Morison's 1942 biography, *Admiral of the Ocean Sea: A Life of Christopher Columbus,* to learn that this same prayer was recited by the men on Columbus's ships as they crossed the Atlantic. There are many other prayers and sayings that people call upon during the course of the day. The daily greeting here is still *Buenos dias le de Dios,* "May God grant you a good day." In planning an activity or looking forward to an event a person might say *Dios mediante* or *Si Dios es servido,* both meaning "God willing." When things turn out well one thanks God with *Gracias a Dios* or *Con el favor de Dios.* When the results are disappointing, one laments *Sea por Dios,* "It is God's will." And when things get really bad this becomes

vii

an expressive *Válgame Dios,* "God help us." **P**rayer enters into every undertaking and often makes its way to God through the intercession of saints. Among the saints most frequently invoked are *San Isidro Labrador,* patron of farmers, and Santa Barbara and San Geronimo for protection from storms and lightning. San Antonio is kept busy finding lost things. It is common for an Hispanic family to have its own special family of saints in the form of statues and paintings on shelves and walls throughout the home. Each time a family member needs a favor from God, he or she prays to the image of the saint. **I** can still remember one day as a child when my mother decided to take the saints down so she could give the walls in our house a thorough scrubbing. She had not gotten around to putting the saints back on the wall before my little brother needed a prayer answered. Instead of waiting he took a crayon and in big letters wrote "JESUS" on my mother's clean wall! This showed me that people do not view images of saints as mere pieces of wood or plaster. They are the living images of faith. **W**hen a child is born, one of the names given to him or her is often that of the saint of the day. When I was young, news of a birth was announced with the words *Dice mi mama que ya tiene una criada mas a quien mandar,* "Mother says you have a new handmaid at your service." I was the oldest of a large family and remember going to our uncles' homes on lower Canyon Road and Delgado Street to deliver that message whenever a new sibling was born. The response from my relatives was always *Que Dios se las preste por muchos anos,* "May God lend her to them for many years." **I**n today's society this custom might be interpreted as demeaning to a woman, but the message is not to be taken too literally. What we acknowledged through this tradition is that life is a gift from God. We are here on this earth for only a short while, and then we are called back to Him. **T**he faith shared by the Hispanic community is also expressed through a host of marvelous celebrations that accompanies many significant events. Every church is dedicated to a saint, and its *función* (celebration) is held on that saint's feast day. The celebration begins with a Mass and is usually followed with an all-day *fiesta* (party) and an evening dance. Other times of celebration include weddings, baptisms, and first communions. If a person has a special devotion to a particular saint, she or he might hold a *velorio* (wake) at home in honor of that saint. This is a gathering of friends and relatives who spend the evening in prayer, singing old hymns, sharing conversation, and enjoying good native foods. **T**he Hispanic family structure also is a reflection of its religious beliefs. In addition to immediate family members and cousins three or four times removed, the extended family includes godparents and godchildren who are spiritual relatives through baptism or marriage. The parents

Anita Thomas in La Fonda's old courtyard, posing in her new *China Poblana* costume for the 1933 Fiestas. Nora Chávez made this photograph with Anita Thomas's Brownie.

and godparents of a child and the parents of a bride and groom are all known as *compadres* (coparents). Before embarking on an important journey or undertaking, it is customary to ask one's parents and godparents for their blessing. **A** wealth of other important customs also evokes the wisdom and fun-loving character of the culture. *Corridos* (ballads), *cuentos* (stories), *decimas romances* (romantic verses), *adivinanzas* (riddles), and nursery rhymes are all rich forms of entertainment for adults and children alike. The myriad *dichos* (sayings) and *refranes* (proverbs) distill the knowledge of the people and add color and wit to their native Spanish language. **T**he lore of Hispanic New Mexico is vast and intriguing. Fortunately, much of it, as well as recipes for the native foods that have sustained the Hispanic people for centuries, has been collected and documented in books. Now, with *Spanish New Mexico: The Spanish Colonial Arts Society Collection,* we have another important resource describing our way of life and the expressions of family and faith that have been shared through the centuries by our *gente* (people) in our *patria chica* (homeland). **I** became involved with the Spanish Colonial Arts Society more than twenty-five years ago when I volunteered my services in helping the organization encourage native artisans to continue the artistic traditions of their Hispanic ancestors. In 1982 I was honored to join the Society's board of directors. I resigned from the board in 1991 after nearly ten years of service but continue to work as a volunteer at many of the organization's events. **D**uring my years with the Society I have been proud to see what I believe is a renaissance in the number of artists who are working to preserve their cultural heritage by perpetuating traditional arts and crafts. Such artists with wonderful talent and sincere commitment have been helped along by the Society's many programs and especially its incredible collection of Spanish colonial materials. For years the collection of the Spanish Colonial Arts Society has provided an invaluable historical and artistic resource for hundreds of native Hispanic artists. With the publication of this important and beautiful book, the knowledge and beauty of Spanish New Mexico can be shared ever more widely. **F**or myself, the Hispanic people of New Mexico, and the Spanish Colonial Arts Society, this book literally represents a dream come true. It was the dream that was brought to New Mexico in 1598 by Don Juan de Oñate and his followers, who transplanted their deep spiritual and family ties in hopes that they would grow and flourish in their new home. Their success is obvious in the Hispanic culture that continues to thrive in New Mexico today. Family and faith are things that never go out of style. **M**any thanks to all who have helped make this dream come true. In the words of the old ones, *Muchas gracias y Dios se los pague,* "Thank you and may God repay you."

PREFACE

The two-volume *Spanish New Mexico: The Spanish Colonial Arts Society Collection* features some six hundred of the Society's more than twenty-five hundred pieces and contextualizes a range of traditional and contemporary Hispanic arts. The Spanish Colonial Arts Society was begun in 1925 by a small group of Santa Feans led by writer Mary Austin and artist Frank G. Applegate. Its certificate of incorporation was signed on October 15, 1929, the same day that the Society purchased El Santuario de Chimayó and entrusted it to the Archdiocese of Santa Fe. Applegate died in 1931, and the organization languished following Austin's death in 1934. It was dormant until the early 1950s, when artist E. Boyd began successful revitalization efforts, later joined by Alan C. Vedder, a collector who learned to restore wooden artifacts, and, when he married, by his wife Ann Healy Vedder. E. Boyd died in 1974, and it was largely through the energies of Alan and Ann Vedder, both of whom died in 1989, that the Society continued to grow and to fulfill the basic tenets of its 1929 incorporation: the encouragement and promotion of Spanish colonial arts; their collection, exhibition, and preservation; and publications and public education related to them. The first items in the collection were acquired by Frank G. Applegate before 1929, but the bulk of them, all but thirty-five, was secured after 1951. The collection's greatest strength is in New Mexico of the colonial period and the nineteenth century, with comparative objects from Spain, Latin America, the Caribbean, the Philippines, and Goa, the Portuguese colony off the coast of India; Catholic religious imagery from non-Hispanic countries; and examples that may have been imported to New Mexico from New England or from other countries, especially China. Numerous twentieth-century pieces from both the revival period of the 1920s and 1930s and the contemporary, post-1965 florescence of Hispanic arts in New Mexico, particularly ones inspired by historic objects in the Society's or museum collections, are also included. Because of its broad scope, the collection of the Spanish Colonial Arts Society supports investigation of a number of historical, contemporary, and comparative themes, and it is the purpose of these two volumes to highlight a range of these objects and to explore their historical context. The first volume, *The Arts of Spanish New Mexico*, opens with an overview of the Hispanic world, and New Mexico in particular, during the colonial, Mexican, and territorial periods until roughly the time of statehood in 1912. The arts are covered generically, from the religious through the mundane: saints, furniture, straw appliqué, precious metals, tin crafts, utilitarian implements, and historical textiles. The second volume, *Hispanic Arts in the Twentieth Century*, proceeds chronologically from the historical overview of the period and brief history of the Society through the arts and artists of the first revival during the 1920s and 1930s to the development of Spanish Market, especially after its 1965 revival, concluding with portraits of several contemporary masters of traditional Hispanic art, most of whom exhibited or still exhibit at the summer and winter markets. A brief history of the collection of the Spanish Colonial Arts Society and notes on its utilization at the Museum of International Folk Art in Santa Fe are appended to volume 2.

ACKNOWLEDGMENTS

DEDICATED TO ALAN AND ANN VEDDER

During the mid-1980s William Field, Ann H. Vedder, and Alan C. Vedder conceived the idea of publishing a book that would make available to the public the collection of the Spanish Colonial Arts Society. They came to consider the project "our museum on paper." The Vedders launched fund-raising efforts to support work on such a publication. **A**lan Vedder and Donna Pierce began reinventory and redocumentation work in late 1988. Pierce started a series of taped interviews with the Vedders early in January 1989. Ann Vedder died on January 24, and Alan Vedder intensified his efforts to complete the book in her memory. He, Pierce, and Museum of International Folk Art Curator Robin Farwell Gavin began a hands-on, photodocumentation inventory of the Society's collection in October 1989. Alan Vedder died on December 8, 1989, and the Society continued the book project in honor of both Vedders. With able and generous assistance from Society volunteer and board member Sandra Osterman, Pierce completed the bulk of the inventory by 1992. **D**onna Pierce succeeded Alan Vedder as the Society's curator in 1990 and began manuscript writing in 1991. Soon thereafter knowledgeable Society members were invited to contribute contextual essays to the project. In 1992, coeditor Marta Weigle started work structuring and copyediting the essays. Jack Parsons began photographing pieces in the collection in 1993. **T**he Publications Committee of the Spanish Colonial Arts Society has overseen this complex project. Between 1989 and 1996 the following members have served various terms on this committee: Teresa Archuleta-Sagel, William Ashbey, Fred Cisneros, William Field, Kay Harvey, Don Madtson, Carmella Padilla, Jack Parsons, Joyce Peters, Donna Pierce, Bud Redding, Anita Gonzales Thomas, Nancy Hunter Warren, and Marta Weigle. Special acknowledgment is due William Ashbey, William Field, and Jack Parsons for their energy and commitment. **I**ncluded in the Ann and Alan Vedder Estate bequeathed to the Spanish Colonial Arts Society was their private collection of about five hundred examples of Hispanic art and material culture. The Vedder collection brought the Society's holdings to some twenty-five hundred pieces, all but thirty-five collected since 1951, primarily under the guidance of E. Boyd and Alan Vedder, and acquired through the generosity of numerous Hispanic families, private collectors, board members, and other interested persons. It was the shared vision of E. Boyd, Alan C. Vedder, and Ann Healy Vedder that shaped the collection's distinct personality, and it is to their memory that this presentation of the Spanish Colonial Arts Society collection—its "museum on paper"—is dedicated.

1. Historical Introduction

1. Reverse of Santa Fe Chamber of Commerce stationery, 1940s. Designed by Wilfred Stedman.

In no other state of this union is the trend of life so clearly shaped by art as in New Mexico.

Art has rescued this state from the commonplace and made it conscious of

its own fine character. . . . In arousing in the minds of our people consciousness of

the beauty of this southwestern land, in restoring this heritage of history,

tradition, poetry, folk life, a priceless service is rendered to our state and its people.

—Edgar Lee Hewett, "Artists and Writers: A List of Prominent Artists
and Writers of New Mexico," special issue of the *Santa Fe New Mexican,* June 26, 1940[1]

New Mexico achieved statehood on January 6, 1912. On August 28 of that year its capital's Chamber of Commerce commissioned "New-Old Santa Fe Style," an exhibition with a twofold purpose: "1st. To awaken local interest in the preservation of the Old Santa Fe and the development of the New along the lines most appropriate to this country. 2nd. To advertise the unique and unrivalled possibilities of the city as 'THE TOURIST CENTER OF THE SOUTHWEST.'" When the exhibition opened on November 18, 1912, it included two important renderings: Sylvanus G. Morley's model of the proposed reconstruction of the *portal* (porch) on the Palace of the Governors "as it might have looked in the mid-1770s" and a watercolor rendering of the Colorado Supply Company Warehouse in Morley, Colorado, designed by the Trinidad, Colorado, architectural firm of brothers I. H. (Isaac Hamilton) and W. M. (William Morris) Rapp. The latter had been solicited by Sylvanus Morley because "the thing is so absolutely in the spirit of 'The Santa Fe Style.'" Morley had also requested examples of work from Kansas City architect Louis Curtiss, who in 1910 designed the Atchison, Topeka & Santa Fe Railway and Fred Harvey Company's El Ortiz hotel at the Lamy, New Mexico, depot. Morley wrote Curtiss on September 14, 1912: "As the circular letter states this Exhibition Management is unanimous in regarding El Ortiz as the best exponent of Santa Fe Style as applied to modern construction."[2] By 1912 the Museum of New Mexico, established by an act of the territorial legislature in 1909, shared the Palace of the Governors with the Historical Society of New Mexico. The historical society had been inaugurated in 1859 and had been an occupant of the Palace since 1882, along with the Archaeological Institute of America's School of American Archaeology (later School of American Research), which was begun in 1907 and had occupied the Palace since 1909. Archaeologist Edgar Lee Hewett served as first director of both the Museum of New Mexico and the School of American Archaeology. On his staff were archaeologist

MARTA WEIGLE

Sylvanus G. Morley, manual arts teacher and photographer Jesse Nusbaum, and painter Carlos Vierra. All four men played significant roles in the development of what Christopher Wilson defines as the Spanish Pueblo Revival, a product of Anglo newcomers to New Mexico between 1904 and 1921.[3] Jesse Nusbaum oversaw interior renovations to the Palace of the Governors between 1909 and 1912. These were hampered by historical society president L. Bradford Prince, who perceived this as encroachment by Hewett, the school, and the museum. Prince refused access to the society's rooms and collections in the Palace until a 1916 illness forced him to relinquish control, and his successor, Santa Fe attorney-historian Ralph Emerson Twitchell, proved more receptive to rapprochement. Prince also served as statutory agent and president of a new preservation group, which he likely used in his fight. On January 15, 1913, he had joined seventy-two signatories, including Archbishop J. B. Pitaval, Amado Chaves, Albert B. Fall, Benjamin M. Read, Bronson M. Cutting, José D. Sena, Camilo Padilla, Venceslao Jaramillo, T. D. Burns, Antonio Lucero, and Felix Martínez, who witnessed a certificate of incorporation for the Society for the Preservation of Spanish Antiquities in New Mexico, claiming as the group's object "the protection and preservation of churches, buildings, landmarks, places and articles of historic interest connected with the Spanish and Mexican occupation of New Mexico."[4] Remodeling the Palace exterior in 1913 was influenced by Sylvanus Morley's 1912 rehabilitation of his Santa Fe adobe house in what he called Spanish style, including an added *portal*. The Palace's Territorial-style porch with its classical embellishments was similarly replaced by a portal supposed to have been part of the structure in the eighteenth century. E. Boyd calls this a "fictional portal," and Wilson emphasizes that the facade is not an example of Spanish Colonial architecture but "an important step in the development and popularization of a regional revival" typified by "a new emphasis on Spanish domestic forms. . .between

1912 and 1915."[5] **I**n 1915 Morley distinguished "California Mission Architecture" from "Santa Fe Architecture," which he defines "as the blending of sixteenth-century Spanish and Indian building practices in an environment, the physical demands of which are exceedingly coercive," with some changes due to "modern living requirements . . . made in the interests of habitability, which Santa Fe dwellings never enjoyed before." He lists five identifying characteristics: (1) "low and long" buildings primarily of one story, never three; (2) horizontal "prominent façade lines" with "flat or very slightly sloping roofs"; (3) facades relieved by "inset porches (*portales*), balconies

2. Portal of the Palace of the Governors and plaza, 1912, Santa Fe, New Mexico.
3. Reconstruction work on the portal of the Palace of the Governors, October 16, 1913, Santa Fe, New Mexico.
4. Roque Lobato residence before Sylvanus G. Morley rehabilitated it, 1912, Santa Fe, New Mexico.
5. Sylvanus G. Morley house after remodeling, 1912, Santa Fe, New Mexico.

(*balcones*), projecting roof-beams and water-spouts (*vigas* and *canales*), . . . and flanking buttresses''; (4) ''color preferably. . .one of the numerous shades of adobe''; and (5) carved wood, including ''wood capitals, columns, architraves, balustrades, cornices, and doors,'' to figure ''extensively and effectively. . .in façade decoration.'' Morley concentrates on exteriors, suggesting only that ''the tendency in interior furnishings should be toward simplicity, best attained by Mission backgrounds'' and that ''although by no means essential, the best results have been obtained by leaving the roof beams (*vigas*) exposed.'' He does picture and discuss a number of corbels and two carved chests because of ''the prominence of wood carving in Santa Fe Architecture.''[6] Morley's colleague Carlos Vierra stressed the Pueblo influence on Franciscan mission architecture. Wilson speculates that ''Morley's emphasis on the Spanish contribution probably resulted from his focusing on Santa Fe architecture and possibly also from the fact that the Museum's annual budget and the funds for the rehabilitation of the Palace of the Governors and the construction of the new museum building came from the Hispanically controlled state legislature.'' Vierra, on the other hand, was very much taken with the rhetoric and representation in the San Diego Panama–California Exposition in 1915–16. At Hewett's behest, he completed ''six mural paintings of the Maya cities Chichen Itza, Uxhual, Copan, Tikal, Quirigua. . . and Palenque'' for that world's fair's California Building.[7] Vierra and Kenneth Chapman were also chosen by Hewett to finish the Saint Francis mural project begun by artist Donald Beauregard before his death in 1914. The six oil paintings had been intended for the New Mexico Building at San Diego but eventually were hung in that structure's Santa Fe replication, the Museum of New Mexico's Fine Arts Museum. Vierra completed three paintings: *Vision of Columbus at La Rábida, Preaching to the Mayas and the Aztecs,* and *Building of the Missions in New Mexico.* Carl Sheppard claims: ''The Saint Francis murals of Santa Fe subtly reveal many of the cultural aspirations prevalent in that small New Mexico town just before the United States joined the Allies during the First World War. . . .[Their] message is one of optimism, of place in a paradise for man, of the dominance of the white civilization of Europe, perfected in America.''[8] The Panama Canal was completed in August 1914 and World War I had begun in Europe before the opening of San Francisco's larger, more global Panama–Pacific International Exposition of 1915 and San Diego's smaller, more regional Panama–California Exposition in 1915 and 1916. The latter was done in Mission Revival architecture at the newly built Balboa Park, where the visitor entered ''the rose trellised gateway and—presto!. . . has stepped backward three or four centuries, full into a city of Old Spain, sprang by magic, domed, towered, castellated, from the top of the mesa.'' San Diego's exposition focused ''on exhibits from Latin America and the American Southwest and on 'a synopsis of man's evolution through a demonstration of the myriad processes which mark the present acme of civilization, and embody the history of man.' ''

Anthropology was its ''linchpin,'' and in 1911 Museum of New Mexico director Edgar Lee Hewett was appointed to mount in the California Building archaeological and ethnological exhibits that would become part of a permanent museum, later incorporated as the San Diego Museum and in 1942 as the Museum of Man.[9] Early in 1913 New Mexico responded enthusiastically to an invitation to participate in the San Diego exposition. The legislature authorized thirty thousand dollars ''for the collection, arrangement, and display of the products of the state of New Mexico at the Panama–California International Exposition at San Diego.'' A Board of Exposition Managers was appointed, and the five-man group elected Ralph Emerson Twitchell to serve as chairman. Among the tangible results of his tenure were the exposition's New Mexico Building and a 256-page illustrated book, *New Mexico The Land of Opportunity: Official Data on the Resources and Industries of New Mexico—The Sunshine State.*[10] The architect brothers I. H. and W. M. Rapp were engaged to create San Diego's New Mexico Building. They had designed New Mexico's temporary pavilion at the 1904 Louisiana Purchase Exposition in St. Louis. It was done in California Mission Revival style, but their San Diego structure resembled Spanish missions at the pueblos, with the general plan based on Acoma's mission church. When the San Diego building was reproduced in 1916 for the Museum of New Mexico's Fine Arts Museum on the Santa Fe plaza near the Palace of the Governors, its inaugural 1917 brochure, *Temple of St. Francis and the Martyrs, The New Museum of Santa Fé,* identified six Franciscan mission churches in the design: Acoma, San Felipe, Cochiti, Laguna, Santa Ana, and Pecos, and applauded all ''the enthusiasts who are planning to make Santa Fé 'different,' to keep it thoroughly primitive in appearance, as befits so historic and ancient a community, [with] the adaptability of the New Mexico mission to every modern building purpose.'' According to Christopher Wilson, ''the churches of Santa Fe, whose Spanish Colonial appearances were known through early photographs and drawings, were overlooked as models for the museum building and ultimately were excluded from the Spanish–Pueblo Revival style. . .[because they] had been built or remodeled late in the Spanish era and as a result had multi-tiered towers, much like those of the California Missions of the same period,''[11] and thus were not distinctive enough for New Mexico's new image. Besides perusing *New Mexico The Land of Opportunity,* visitors to San Diego's New Mexico Building could view exhibits, a film, and stereopticon pictures of the state. They might also pick up a special issue of the *Santa Fe New Mexican* extolling the virtues of what one contributor, W. N. Townsend, called the Granada of America, the ''City of a Thousand Wonders.'' These exposition displays were part of a concerted tourism promotion because, Wilson indicates,

Santa Fe had been in a gradual decline since being by-passed by the main line of the Santa Fe Railroad in 1880, losing approximately ten per cent of its population each decade from 1880 to 1910. The development of mining and light

4

7. Postcard of the New Mexico Building exterior at the Panama–California Exposition, 1915.

New Mexico Building, Panama California Exposition, San Diego, 1915.

6. Interior patio of the New Mexico Building at the Panama–California Exposition, 1915, San Diego, California.
8. Room in the New Mexico Building at the Panama–California Exposition, 1915, San Diego, California.

industry, the introduction of modern farming techniques and the establish-
ment of a tubercular sanitarium had simply not compensated for the loss of the
city's standing as the Southwest's leading mercantile center. The development
of tourism was finally grasped as a way to stem this decline.[12]

Ruth Laughlin Barker vividly captures this boosterism in a 1916 article for *Sunset*, "Keeping the Oldest Capital Old: How the Hard-Headed Business Men of Santa Fe Met the Demands of Americans Who Had to See America First." Those Americans

saw the chapel of San Miguel, the oldest church in the United States, and
examined the arrow holes in the paintings made when the Indians rebelled in
1680. They took a tape line and assured themselves that the walls in the adobe
houses were really five feet thick. They used impressionistic superlatives for the
doors and window sills painted a Virgin Mary blue. They glanced through
the doorways into placitas where the sunshine fell upon tall hollyhocks, Sweet
William and the bright-hued family wash. They followed old women in black
shawls up crooked streets until they crossed a narrow plank over a creek where
children were wading. They stopped burros laden with wood and paid more for
taking the picture than the wood was worth. They insisted that the street scenes
and the blue skies were transported from Spain and found in the dark-eyed
Spanish girls types in which Zuloaga reveled.

Their cry, "Don't change this bit of Old Spain," meant that "the ancient city whitened her hair, drew crows feet under her eyes, pulled a rusty black shawl over her head and posed for the world to come and see her as the oldest capital in the United States, the royal headquarters for the Kingdom of Spain for one hundred and fifty years before the Mexican War, and since then the capital of the state of New Mexico."[13]

Santa Fe's so-called "revived" Fiesta in 1919 renewed concerns for the city's historicity. While acknowledging the city's religious observances celebrating Diego de Vargas's 1692–93 "Reconquest of the Southwest from the Pueblo Indians" as going back to 1712, members of Santa Fe's "comparatively small business community" tried to find a way to restore the occasional "secular pageants and fiestas" mounted in the Tertio-Millennial celebration of 1883 and more recently at the time of statehood in order "to stage a pageant worthy of the traditions of the Capital." Edgar Lee Hewett suggested that a pageant was not nearly unique enough for Santa Fe and that "in a Fiesta, the entire populace is a part of the celebration, and when a populace is as varied, as picturesque, as that of Santa Fe, that in itself furnishes the substantial basis for a colorful, distinctive and noteworthy event." Accordingly, on September 11, 12, and 13, "the civic organizations" staged a "three days' 'Fiesta,' the first day to be given to the Indians or to the days 'Before Santa Fe Was,' the second day to the Spanish culture transplanted to New Mexico or 'Santa Fe Antigua,' while the third day was to be given to 'Santa Fe Moderna,' with a formal welcome to the 17,000 and more men from New Mexico who served in the Great War."[14] **T**he second day included the revived de Vargas pageant, a costumed

reenactment of his entry into Santa Fe that had first been mounted during the Tertio-Millennial celebration in 1883, next during 1911 Independence Day festivities, and most recently for the Fourth of July celebration following statehood. Thomas E. Chávez reports that "George Armijo played the role of Diego de Vargas for the third time... [and he] and *su cuadrilla* (his troop) marched along the by-then traditional route from Rosario to the plaza where, in front of the Palace, Armijo read a long proclamation." Genuine Franciscans also marched with the troop and later conducted a mass and vespers, followed by "the first candlelight procession to the Cross of the Martyrs in memory of those priests who lost their lives during the Pueblo Revolt."[15] **I**n 1925, the year that the Spanish Colonial Arts Society was founded, Edgar Lee Hewett announced that the August 4–8 "Fiesta of Santa Fe, the Epic of the Southwest," was "under the auspices of the School of American Research, which aims to make it an exposition of the history and civilization of the Southwest throughout the ages," including "THE SOUTHWEST of Today Where the Glories of Old Spain, the Romance of Old Mexico, the Life of Ancient America Survive in the Pageantry, Drama, Music and Art of Old Santa Fe." Among the published *Papers of the School of American Research* in 1925 is *The Fiesta Book*, a hundred-page compilation with the stated "purpose...to assemble for future use the material that has been prepared for the celebrations of the last few years...[covering] only the essential historical and ethnological material." Included is the script of a three-part "Historic Pageant, New Mexico Across the Centuries," by Edgar L. Hewett, F. S. Curtis, Jr., and Lansing B. Bloom. In the Fiesta of 1927 this public drama became the "Pageant of Old Santa Fe" and was directed by Thomas Wood Stevens of Chicago.[16] **P**rior to Santa Fe's civic promotional campaigns, Hispanic longevity in the Southwest had been capitalized for the most part by the Atchison, Topeka and Santa Fe Railway and its close associate, the Fred Harvey Company, both of which used *conquistador* imagery in their development of tourism in the region along the way between Chicago and California. Founded in 1868 by Colonel Cyrus K. Holliday, the Kansas-based AT and SF Railroad reached the New Mexico border in December 1878, Las Vegas in July 1879, Galisteo Junction (later Lamy) and Santa Fe via a branch line in February 1880, and Albuquerque in April of that year. Track went to Holbrook, Arizona, in September 1881, and a West Coast connection was established at Needles, California, in August 1883, when the Santa Fe met the Southern Pacific. English immigrant Frederick Henry Harvey opened his first railroad-connected lunchroom at Topeka, Kansas, in 1876 and signed on January 1, 1878, the first formal contract for train and trackside accommodations between the Fred Harvey Company and the Santa Fe Railroad. Following the depression of 1893, the Santa Fe Railroad faced bankruptcy and receivership and was reorganized as the Atchison, Topeka and Santa Fe Railway late in 1895. It soon prospered under its first and longtime president, Edward P. Ripley, who immediately began promoting the struggling operation

9. De Vargas *Entrada* participants, Tertio-Millennial celebration, 1883, Santa Fe, New Mexico.

10. Enactment of de Vargas *Entrada* enters the plaza, Fiesta, August 2–8, 1925, Santa Fe, New Mexico.

with advertising campaigns focused on the natural wonderland of the Grand Canyon and the colorful life of the region's Pueblo and Navajo peoples.[17] The first AT and SF depots were standardized, wood-frame structures, some of which were replaced in the late 1890s by Mission Style, brick-and-masonry buildings, often with nearby station-hotels to attract and accommodate the growing tourist traffic. Las Vegas, New Mexico, was one of the first depots to receive such a replacement in 1898; its station-hotel, the Castañeda, opened in January 1899. Named for Coronado's chronicler Pedro de Castañeda by AT&SF president Ripley, it was designed by California architect Frederick L. Roehrig in a Mission Style frame construction veneered with buff brick and a Colonial (American, not Spanish) Revival interior.[18] After 1902 Albuquerque's depot complex became the prototype for the Santa Fe/Harvey "Great Southwest" developed between the Grand Canyon's El Tovar Hotel and Hopi House (1905) and Santa Fe's La Fonda (1926–29). That year, the frame depot was replaced by two structures: a Mission Style wood-stucco building for passengers and a brick-stucco building with wood addition for freight. The nearby station-hotel, the Alvarado, was designed by Los Angeles architect Charles F. Whittlesey, who had trained in the Chicago office of Louis Sullivan and become chief architect for the Santa Fe Railway. According to the 1909 edition of *The Alvarado A New Hotel at Albuquerque, New Mexico, Fred Harvey, The Santa Fe:* "Captain Hernando de Alvarado, Commander of Artillery for Coronado's expedition, was noted for his gallantry at the storming of Cibola. He commanded the first expedition eastward from Cibola, was the first European to visit Acoma, and the old towns where Bernalillo, Taos, and Pecos now stand, [and] returned to Mexico with Coronado in 1542." The Alvarado, billed as "the finest railroad hotel on earth," opened on May 11, 1902, "in a burst of rhetoric, a flow of red carpet and the glow of myriad brilliant electric lights."[19] Two other buildings completed the Albuquerque depot complex: the Indian Museum (or Collection) Building, housing anthropological exhibits and the Fred Harvey Indian Department, and the Indian and Mexican Building on the station platform between the passenger depot and the Alvarado. Mary Colter designed the latter's interior, which contained museum displays, demonstration areas, and salesrooms. An early Fred Harvey brochure for the Indian and Mexican Building describes museum-type exhibits in the Main Room, the Modern Blanket Room, the Pacific Room, and the Spanish and Mexican Room, where there are

antique chimallos [blankets] and serapes, delicate in shade and curious in pattern; old altar cloths and tapestries, many having been in use over two hundred years; relics from churches that have long been in ruins [including "ancient Mission bells," according to a 1909 version of the pamphlet]; old shields and swords; antique Spanish shawls, mantillas and rebosas [shawls]. In addition are the modern serapes, chimallos and scarfs, Mexican drawn linens, laces and filigree silverware [gold as well in 1909].

Christopher Wilson found Mexican filigree jewelry first advertised in Santa Fe in 1878 and soon the "leading souvenir and its production the city's leading industry." Ironically, operations such as the Harvey Company's contributed to its decline around 1915, "when the national popularity of filigree waned . . . , and simultaneously an influx of artists and writers gave increasing attention to local Indians, [so] filigree was displaced in sales by Indian turquoise and silver work."[20] The success of the Indian Building, as it soon came to be called, was due in large part to its manager Herman Schweizer, who served as head of the Fred Harvey News and Curio Department from 1901 until his death in 1943. Best known for his work with Indian arts and their preservation and commercialization in the Harvey system, Schweizer also made buying trips to Mexico and acquired Hispanic pieces there and throughout the Santa Fe/Harvey Southwest. E. Boyd notes, for example: "Agents for the Fred Harvey Indian Company also collected [*santos,* or images of saints] in southern New Mexico, and in all cases little or no record was kept of the place of origin of the examples."[21] Schweizer became friends with Mary Austin several years before her death and worked with the Spanish Colonial Arts Society. In April 1936 Albuquerque field writer Janet Smith interviewed Herman Schweizer for the New Mexico Federal Writers' Project and reported:

When I asked Mr. Herman Schweitzer [sic] to show me the Harvey Collection of santos, he said that he had never pretended to make a collection,—merely had a few unusual objects which were put away in a vault and not offered for sale. He unlocked the heavy doors of the vault and left me alone in a small room full of baskets, Indian jewelry and costumes and santos, remarking that he had never had time to make a study of santos and no one knew much about them anyhow. He would come in every few minutes to see how I was getting along and point out some particularly rare object.

Smith describes the following *bultos* (sculptures): "a rather large [one] of Saint Louis, which Mr. Schweitzer [sic] said he believed to be the only one of that particular saint in existence among the Spanish-American santos"; "a small santo with inset glass eyes, which he said was a very unusual object and probably came from Old Mexico"; "two ivory santos about a foot in height, . . . very rare"; three "Guadalupe Virgins"; two Our Lady of Sorrows; two Saint Isidore's; "San Miguel, a beardless youth over two feet high with huge wings and a pair of scales"; an unidentified saint carrying a child, the former with "a stalwart, blond and Nordic face with high forehead and close cropped hair, very different from the usual swarthy, triangular and mustachioed Spanish faced santo"; "a man nailed to the cross, possibly San Acacio, [with] six small figures carved at the base"; and "San Domingo which Mr. Schweitzer [sic] said was rare." The *retablos* (paintings on wood) include San Jose, on which "at the bottom was written: San Jose 1823, and Mr. Schweitzer said it was the only santo he had ever seen that bore a name and a date"; Saint Raphael; Saint Rita; Our Lady of the Rosary;

11. Fred Harvey Company postcard of its Castañeda Hotel, Las Vegas, New Mexico.
12. Fred Harvey Company postcard of its Alvarado Hotel, Albuquerque, New Mexico.
13. Fred Harvey Company postcard of the Spanish room in the Indian Building near the Alvarado Hotel, Albuquerque, New Mexico.
14. Spanish room in the Indian Building, Albuquerque, New Mexico.

Guadalupe Virgin; Virgin and Child "painted with a rather unusual blue in the mantle and rich reds"; and in a drawer "a tiny Guadalupe Virgin painted on shell, and a small figure of San Rafael with a large head crudely painted on paper under glass." There was also "a very interesting old oil painting done on wood" that appeared to be a Spanish "portrait of a young woman" and about which Schweizer "said he knew absolutely nothing...some native had brought it in, but he judged that it had come originally from Spain." As Smith was leaving, Schweizer "called my attention to a drawer full of old Spanish shawls, two rare ones embroidered on black lace" and "a remarkable straw portrait of Pope Pius IX, a framed santo made entirely of beads of the Lamb of Saint George, found in a church in Old Mexico."[22] An undated report describes Smith's visit to the Fred Harvey Indian Building:

In the room next to the Hopi room are a number of santos, bultos and retablos, ranging in price from a few dollars to $65.00. They appear to be less rare and of inferior workmanship to those in the private Harvey collection. In this same room is...a pair of six-foot candlesticks, bought by Fred Harvey in one of the old churches of Mexico, after the Revolution of 1912,—not for sale. There is a large carved table, originally from Alcalde, and an excellent example of early Spanish woodcarving. On the table stands a big pot, made of old hand wrought copper, picked up somewhere in this State. Almost all of one side of the room is occupied by an old wagon of Spanish days, acquired by Fred Harvey, in 1906 from Santa Fe where it had stood for many years on top of the former Jake Gold curio shop....In this same room are two cabinets, carved and fashioned of white mountain pine by the early Spanish wood carvers. One of them is very fine and is not for sale. In this same room are native malls, swords and daggers picked up from various early settlers.

Since the late 1870s Jake Gold had operated his Free Museum and Curiosity Shop on San Francisco Street. To attract tourists, when he expanded the store in 1893, he mounted the *carreta* (cart) on the roof, employed an Indian clerk, hired Mexican weavers to demonstrate their skills inside, and staged Indian dances in the courtyard. The *Santa Fe New Mexican* also noted that the *portal* and "the ancient style of the interior finish will be preserved, as the curio dealer thinks it would be vandalism to modernize the house considering he intends to dub it the 'old curio shop.'"[23]

The Santa Fe/Harvey system began to incorporate Hispanic elements in its interior decoration in 1910, when Kansas City architect Louis Curtiss designed El Ortiz hotel next to the Lamy depot, which had been converted from a wood-frame to a brick-stucco structure in 1909. David Gebhard considers El Ortiz, which was razed in 1943, "outstanding" and "unquestionably the most romantic and in certain ways the most eclectic [of the Santa Fe/Harvey Houses] with its false

15. Interior of La Fonda Hotel, ca. 1926–29, Santa Fe, New Mexico.

vega [*sic*] ceiling, its portal and completely enclosed court yard." Mary Colter designed the interior of the one-story building, which Virginia L. Grattan describes:

It was a small inn, having fewer than ten rooms. The lounge had the traditional log-beam viga ceiling and a fireplace on which Colter created a geometric Indian design in the brickwork. She furnished the lounge with a heavy carved Mexican table surrounded by brass-studded, straight-backed chairs. The table held a large fern in an Indian pot, and the tile floor was covered with Navajo rugs. On one wall hung a large Mexican retablo....; against another stood a large carved Spanish chest.[24]

La Fonda on the Santa Fe plaza became the foremost example of the Santa Fe/Harvey system's use of Hispanic ambiance. Other hotels had stood on that spot, but the current structure began in 1920 as the last major commission of I. H. and W. M. Rapp and A. C. Hendrickson, Architects, who adapted the Lincoln Avenue facade of their Museum of Fine Arts for the hotel. The new La Fonda went into receivership in 1922; the Santa Fe Railway bought it in 1925 and leased it to the Fred Harvey Company in 1926. John Gaw Meem was commissioned to modify and enlarge the Rapps' design, and by July 1927 he had established his own: "The exterior of the hotel will be in the Spanish-Pueblo style...[with] the emphasis...more on mass than ornament. Its numerous set backs and ornaments will recall the terracing in the more ancient Pueblos of Taos and Acoma."[25] Mary Colter oversaw the interior decoration, which was predominantly Mexican and New Mexican, producing an effect that at the official reopening was heralded by the *Santa Fe New Mexican* of May 18, 1929, as: "La Fonda, Tripled in Size Becomes Spanish Fairyland."

The Harvey House's inaugural 1929 brochure, *La Fonda in Old Santa Fé: The Inn at the End of the Trail,* extols the atmosphere of the "guest rooms and suites, where spaciousness and simplicity are enhanced by the use of paintings by Pueblo Indian artists, antique pieces imported from Spain, and other furniture especially developed from the finest examples of Spanish-American craft." Grattan claims Colter's redecoration produced

an informal, warm, primarily Mexican decor. Every piece of furniture in the guest rooms, lounges, portales..., patio, lecture room, and cabaret was made according to her specifications. The furniture was shipped from Kansas City unfinished, and Colter brought Kansas City artist Earl Altaire to Santa Fe to hand paint it. He hand painted 798 pieces after Colter worked out the design and color scheme for each room on a separate sheet of paper.[26]

Each of La Fonda's 156 rooms was unique in design and color scheme.

16. Hotel El Ortiz, 1912,
Lamy, New Mexico.

19. Patio of La Fonda Hotel,
ca. 1930, Santa Fe, New Mexico.

17. Patio of Hotel El Ortiz,
1912, Lamy, New Mexico.

20. Suite in La Fonda Hotel,
ca. 1926–29, Santa Fe, New Mexico.

18. Fred Harvey postcard of the lobby
of its Hotel El Ortiz, Lamy, New Mexico.

21. Woodvendor's burros in
front of Gold's Old Curiosity Shop, San Francisco
Street, Santa Fe, New Mexico.

Although the furnishings were not locally made, the light fixtures were. A 1930 brochure enthuses:

The prevalence of things in tin adds to the spirit of originality pervading the hotel. Tin nichos [niches] and sconces, candlesticks, light shades and cords and even the unique frames of plate glass mirrors all are the painstaking work of Mexican artists. Scores of hand wrought Spanish lanterns hang in the portales, the Lecture Lounge, and the halls.

22. Cover of Fred Harvey Company/Santa Fe Railway Indian Detours brochure, 1927.

The Lecture Lounge, "in form a New Mexican chapel, with high carved doors, great fireplace, bancos and balcony," served by day as "another lounge, with huge chairs and couches and subdued richness in drapes and glowing rugs" and at night as site of Indian Detours' "informal illustrated talks on that Southwest of which the hotel is so fascinating an embodiment."[27] **L**a Fonda was the center for the newly formed Santa Fe/Harvey Indian Detours, chauffeured car tours with specially trained Courier "girl" guides who enabled railroad tourists to see "the beckoning, foot-loose distances of New Mexico and Arizona . . . [and to] find out . . . buried cities that flourished when Britons crouched in caves, reach medieval Spain dreaming away the centuries in the mountains of America, and string together age-old Indian pueblos where one may 'catch archaeology alive.'" The first three-day tour was launched on May 15, 1926. Detourists, called dudes, disembarked from the train at either Albuquerque or Las Vegas and spent the first day touring ruins, pueblos, and villages on the way to Santa Fe, staying overnight at La Fonda. On the second day they visited Puyé Cliffs, Santa Clara Pueblo, and Tesuque Pueblo; toured Santa Fe; and heard an evening lecture at La Fonda. The third day included more ruins, pueblos, and villages on the way to rejoin the train at either Las Vegas or Albuquerque. Like most later Detours, the first ones concentrated on prehistoric ruins and contemporary Indians, with only some stops in Hispanic villages. Tourists in 1926, for example, visited Tecolote, San José, and, for some passengers arriving on The Navajo in Albuquerque the day before, "afternoon motor drives about Albuquerque, including Mexican villages."[28] **C**órdova became a regular stop on some later Indian Detours. It had already attracted Frank Applegate, Mary Austin, and others, according to Charles L. Briggs:

José Dolores Lopez was "discovered" by leading members of the Spanish Colonial Arts Society shortly after 1921. Austin, Applegate, and their friends frequented Cordova during Holy Week. . . . Lorin Brown, born in [Elizabethtown] of a [Taos] Mexicana mother and an Anglo-American father, was living in Cordova. Being bilingual and well-acquainted with both Mexicano and Anglo-American cultures, Brown proved the perfect mediator between Cordovans and the artists and writers who were his guests. . . . Brown introduced Applegate to Lopez, and Applegate acquainted Lopez with Mary Austin. They soon persuaded Lopez to exhibit his carvings in Santa Fe, and he won first prize for a wall rack in the carved furniture category of the second annual prize competition of Spanish Colonial Arts in 1927.

Applegate and Austin's patronage brought stylistic changes to López's work: from brightly painted and chip-carved ornamentation to chip carving only, production of fewer traditional items and more items for use in Anglo homes such as lazy Susans and record racks, and carvings of "unpainted representations of Catholic holy personages." Briggs notes:

Lopez's patrons later "encouraged" him to carve smaller pieces, suitable for sale to tourists. He accordingly produced birds and animals of all sizes as well as multifigure scenes, such as the animal musicians . . . [and] imitations of Swiss and German toys. . . . He also produced screen doors on commission for Santa Feans such as Mary Austin.[29]

Art colonists Mary Austin and poet Alice Corbin Henderson were featured in a 1928 Santa Fe Railway/Indian Detours booklet entitled *They Know New Mexico: Intimate Sketches by Western Writers.* According to its "Who's Who" notes on the six authors who "know" (Austin, Henderson, Witter Bynner, Eugene Manlove Rhodes, Elizabeth Willis De Huff, and Charles F. Lummis):

Alice Corbin (Mrs. Wm. P. Henderson) came to Santa Fé from Chicago in 1916. She and her artist husband have a picturesque adobe home, of many buildings, on the windswept top of a high mesa overlooking the ancient city and the mountains [on Camino del Monte Sol, called Telephone Road until 1917 when Henderson petitioned to have the Spanish name reinstated], where are carried on the correlated activities of home, studio, literary retreat and the making of hand-carved art furniture. In this casa [home] notables in the literary and art worlds often meet for informal talks and entertainment.[30]

The furniture making was William Penhallow Henderson's. **F**rom 1926 through the early 1930s Henderson designed and produced handmade furniture because, as his wife explained in *House and Garden* magazine:

Of late years the marked renaissance of adobe architecture in New Mexico has occasioned a need of Spanish type furniture in keeping with this simple and elemental architecture; and, the supply of originals being limited, this need has been met by the creation of modern furniture based on old traditions. The furniture renaissance of New Mexico may be said to begin with the artists of Taos and Santa Fe who, having built their own adobe houses, then proceeded, like the early Spanish pioneers, to build the furniture to go in them.

Henderson's shop foreman, house carpenter, and native Santa Fean Gregorio Gabaldón, had not made furniture until his employer taught him how. Alice Corbin notes her husband's "crew of Mexican artisans," whom he "set to work on furniture, for which he supplied the designs as well as the necessary instruction in joining and carving, thus initiating them to the mysteries of their own forgotten craft (so far forgotten, indeed, that most of their own houses were furnished from mail-order catalogues)."[31] Besides three poems for the poetry section of *They Know New Mexico* Alice Corbin contributed a five-page piece, "Old Spain in New Mexico," in which she expresses the art colonists' prevailing fly-in-amber view of those "small sunlit villages of flat-roof adobe houses...[and] Old World charm":

The life in these placitas is almost as simple today as it was of necessity in the days of their settlement; the speech is still that of the Conquistadores, preserving many words long since obsolete in Spain, though current in the pages of Don Quixote....*A three-centuries-old Nativity Play,* Los Pastores, *is performed at Christmas....Every year during Lent, the Penitente Brotherhood (*Los Hermanos Penitentes *or* Los Hermanos de la Sangre de Cristo), *an unorthodox survival of the Third Order of Saint Francis, make religious pilgrimages and processions, including cross-bearing and flagellation—medieval symbols of atonement brought to this country by the first Spanish settlers and priests, and common at that date throughout Europe.*

She also describes "the old New Mexican–Spanish missions" with their "elemental simplicity" and "white-washed interiors, enlivened by painted *retablos* and *santos,* or by beautifully carved wooden Crucifixions or *bultos,* [which] preserve an equally primitive feeling."[32] During the early 1920s Alice Corbin and William Penhallow Henderson witnessed Brotherhood rites at Abiquiú, New Mexico. He illustrated her 1937 account of those occasions in *Brothers of Light: The Penitentes of the Southwest.* At a night procession of crossbearers they felt: "The clock of time had mysteriously turned back. This was not the United States of the Twentieth Century, but the heart of the Middle Ages." Both were impressed by the "small and large *Santos...* [their] crudely carved faces...curiously real and living..., of native craft, the primitive wood sculpture of this country, in which passion and beauty are instinctively chiseled in the crudely painted wooden features." At the end of the Good Friday night *Tinieblas* (Tenebrae) services in the *morada* (chapel/chapterhouse) its leader, the *Hermano Mayor,*

raised his hand, and delivered a short address...in Spanish, but intended for los Americanos *present....We were not to think, he said, that they worshipped—pointing to the images on the altar—these* Muñecas, *these dolls, for themselves. They were the images of the Saints in Heaven; and the ceremonies which we had seen tonight and during the past few days were not savage or barbaric, but were deeply religious mysteries which had been handed down to them by their forefathers from France and Spain.*[33]

Most of the art colonists perpetuated what Suzanne Forrest calls "the

23. Worship in Abiquiú *morada* chapel; woodcut illustration by William Penhallow Henderson for frontispiece to Alice Corbin Henderson, *Brothers of Light: The Penitentes of the Southwest.*

mystique of the village." In New Mexico after 1900, successive "waves of artist-intellectuals . . . , many of them, especially after World War I, reform-minded progressives eager to put their own distinctive stamp upon the state," attempted "to develop the area economically while preserving the 'quaint and picturesque' nature of its native inhabitants," including Hispanic villagers. By the 1930s these "intellectuals, as they saw mainstream American society breaking apart, apparently rotten to the core, were more convinced than ever that the New Mexican village held the key to America's future." Roland F. Dickey too comments on the postwar "concerted effort to gather evidences of dying folkways [and] the Spanish Colonial Revival movement, which had some of the fire of the old-fashioned Methodist Revival, . . . led by Mary Austin, Frank Applegate, and other appreciative souls who recognized the intrinsic beauty of the New Mexican tradition and sought to perpetuate it."[34] The perpetuation and revival of Hispanic New Mexican traditions were also concerns of natives Nina Otero-Warren, who published *Old Spain in Our Southwest* in 1936, and Cleofas Martínez Jaramillo, whose *Shadows of the Past (Sombras del pasado)* appeared in 1941. The latter lamented: "As a descendant of the Spanish pioneers, I have watched with regret the passing of the old Spanish customs and the rapid adoption of the modern Anglo customs by the new generation." In 1935 she had "organized a Spanish Folklore Society," *La Sociedad Folklórica,* because "on account of familiarity with the old customs, we had not awakened to the fact that they were worth preserving, until in recent years, and have turned our effort to revive them."[35] Genaro M. Padilla analyzes Jaramillo's 1955 cultural autobiography, *Romance of a Little Village Girl,* to show that

she understood the exploitative motive underlying the behavior of those new-comers who were infatuated with Nuevomexicano culture. Her almost single-handed organization of La Sociedad Folklórica *in the 1930s must be regarded as a gesture of resistance to Anglo domination of cultural preservation activities in Santa Fe. Although the idea for* La Sociedad *was influenced by similar Anglo folklore preservation projects, specifically J. Frank Dobie's Texas Folklore Society [176], she seized on a decidedly political strategy when forming the group: the romanticized genealogy and melodious language celebrated in* extranjero *discourse about New Mexico would be used to exclude non-natives. Jaramillo writes, "The first rules which I drafted still govern the organization. These rules were that the society should be composed of only thirty members, all of whom must be of Spanish descent, and that the meetings must be conducted in the Spanish language, with the aim of preserving our language, customs and traditions" [176]. Such rules, clearly a form of ethnocodifying, effectively excluded the likes of Austin, [artist Will] Shuster, [poet Witter] Bynner, and other "writers and artists who have come into our country."*

Padilla also notes that "her efforts to 'arouse more interest amongst our Spanish-speaking population in taking part of the [Santa Fe] fiesta' is described as a direct response to cultural activities controlled by Anglo-Americans, she says, because, 'so far we have been seeing

mostly what Americans have arranged' [174]."[36] Charles L. Briggs points out a dilemma in these "arrangements" and the Anglo-dominated revivalist fervor. Most of the early Spanish Colonial Arts Society efforts "were devoted to providing better marketing outlets [and] they accordingly organized exhibitions and markets, selecting work for display and awarding prizes." Thus, Anglo elites, "by deciding who could participate in markets and exhibitions, . . . even determined what was to be defined as 'traditional' *Mexicano* art." These patrons' "object-fetishism"—their failure to comprehend the dynamics of the artisans' complex relationship to craft, community and culture—meant that their "efforts did not 'encourage' the artists to meet the needs of their communities, . . . [but] rather taught [them] profit-oriented marketing strategies and ways of accommodating the newcomers' aesthetic patterns . . . thus ultimately further[ing] the very process of commercialization and cultural homogenization that they decried."[37] The Spanish Colonial Arts Society opened a shop in the Sena Plaza in 1930. A *colcha* (embroidery) adorns its letterhead, which proclaims The Spanish Arts to deal wholesale and retail in "Contemporary Spanish Art of New Mexico: Furniture, Chests, Rugs, Blankets, Carvings, Toys, Ornamental Iron, Ornamental Tin, Painted Glass, Embroideries, Colchas." This exclusive concentration on Hispanic arts made the shaky enterprise unique among Santa Fe establishments such as the venerable Gold/Candelarios'; H. C. Yontz's jewelry store on San Francisco Street, which marketed filigree jewelry and Indian blankets; Julius Gans's plaza Southwest Arts and Crafts shop, with silversmiths and weavers at work on the premises, where both Indian and Spanish crafts were sold; the Old Santa Fe Trading Post on Cathedral Place; La Fonda's Indian Room store and museum display of "old Spanish, Mexican, and Indian handicraft that have been thirty years in the gathering, [including] antique Chimayos and serapes, Spanish shawls, mantillas and rebosos, relics from old churches and missions, Mexican drawn linen and gold and silver filigree"; and the Spanish and Indian Trading Company, first in the Prince Plaza and then north of La Fonda.[38] Some eight months after The Spanish Arts closed on October 10, 1933, Leonora Curtin opened The Native Market on Palace Avenue a block from the Santa Fe plaza on June 16, 1934. Curtin subsidized the venture with an expectation that it would eventually be self-supporting. "Crafts were marked up only 33⅓ percent, to pay for the maintenance of the Market and salaries of craftsmen employed by the shop. Only craft items which met a certain standard were bought . . . , while other items were taken on consignment, but quality was always stressed." Initial stock "included furniture (chairs, tables, beds, chests, *trasteros* [cabinets], and doors); perishable foods as well as dried grains and vegetables; hides (calf, sheep, and goatskins, natural or tinted with vegetable dyes); parchments for lampshades and book bindings; rabbit skins; leather and horsehair reins, quirts, and sets for horses; hand spun and dyed yarns; wool blankets and both rag and wool rugs; *colcha* embroidery and drawn work on tablecloths and napkins; carved

24. Interior of The Spanish Arts shop, Sena Plaza, Santa Fe, New Mexico.

25. Letterhead for The Spanish Arts Shop.

The Spanish Arts

Sena Plaza   Santa Fe, N. M.

Contemporary Spanish Art of New Mexico

Furniture   Ornamental Iron
Chests   Ornamental Tin
Rugs   Painted Glass
Blankets   Embroideries
Carvings   Colchas
Toys

Wholesale and Retail

H. McCrossen, Manager

27. Curio shop in La Fonda Hotel, ca. 1927–28, Santa Fe, New Mexico.

26. Cleofas Martínez Jaramillo (1878–1956) in gown.

wooden trays, candlesticks, toys, *santos, nichos. . . .*, smoking stands, buckles, and buttons; tin light fixtures, mirrors, picture frames, boxes, crosses, and flowerpots; and hand wrought iron locks, latches, hinges, door bolts, pokers, curtainrods, and candlesticks."[39] **B**etween 1934 and the summer of 1937, Sarah Nestor notes:

Craftsmen employed at the Market included Tillie Gabaldon (dyeing and colcha embroidery), Deolinda Baca (colcha embroidery and some weaving), Doña Maria and her daughter Atocha Martinez (carding and spinning), Valentin Rivera, Margaret Baca, and David Salazar (weaving), Pedro Quintana (tinwork), David Lammlae (painting on tin, glass, and furniture), and David Villiaseñor from Mexico (wood carving). . . . In addition Abad Lucero, who made furniture in a back room of his home in Santa Fe, filled furniture orders for The Native Market. Village craftsmen who brought in their goods . . . were given advice and instructions by these experts when they were needed.

The Native Market proved so successful that The Tucson Native Market was opened in 1936, and a mail-order business was begun out of the Santa Fe shop. Twelve employees and some two hundred artisans were associated with the enterprise that year.[40] **T**he Native Market had considerable competition in Santa Fe and elsewhere. Besides the Ortega and Trujillo families in Chimayó, who for years had been marketing their textiles, Santa Fe weaving operations included Preston and Helen McCrossen's Kraft Shop, Celima Padilla's Santa Fe Weavers, the Knox Weavers, Burro Weavers, Southwestern Arts, and R. H. Welton's Southwestern Master Craftsmen, which also offered a range of Hispanic furnishings. Furniture was also available at Eleanor Bedell's Spanish Indian Trading Company and in Taos at Harry Simms's Craft O'Taos Studios. Decorative tinwork could be purchased from Francisco and Eddie Delgado, Francisco Sandoval, and at least four Anglos: Benjamin Sweringen, Bruce Cooper, Majel Claflin, and Robert Woodman, the latter who worked with architects such as John Gaw Meem.[41] **T**his lively commerce and the growing tourist traffic prompted Santa Fe businesspeople to approach Leonora Curtin in the spring of 1937 about re-creating El Parian, Santa Fe's bustling market on Galisteo Street during the 1880s and 1890s. The new El Parian Analco was to be on what was then College Street in two buildings and on land owned by the Salazar family across from San Miguel Mission and St. Michael's College. The complex included The Native Market, a tortilla mill and restaurant, a bar, an open air theater, and a plaza with bandstand and outdoor dance floor surrounded by some thirty booths for crafts and produce. The crafts booths did not flourish and most of that business was carried on through El Parian Native Market. It continued to be subsidized by Curtin, who with Indian Detours head and Chamber of Commerce president Major R. Hunter Clarkson, also led the ten-member Native Market Association, which owned El Parian separately from the shop.[42] **E**l Parian Analco craftspeople were listed in the *Santa Fe Plaza* of August 1, 1937, as:

Weavers—E. D. Trujillo, José Ramon Ortega of Chimayó, the latter in charge of weaving neckties; Alfredo Catanach, Valentin Rivera, Max Ortiz.
Spinners—Donaciana Romero, Lena Barela.
Finishers—Refugio Leyba.
Embroidery—Deolinda Baca.
Tinwork—Eddie Delgado, Pedro Quintana.
Woodworkers—Ben Sandoval, Abad Lucero, Ben Lujan, Ramon Martinez, two boys from Taos.

Most of the Palace Avenue Native Market staff were at the new site in 1937: Tillie Gabaldon, Deolinda Baca, Valentin Rivera, David Lammlae, and Pedro Quintana. They were joined by Filiberto Salazar (weaving), Refugio Leyba (furniture finishing and painting), Eliseo Rodriguez (painting and leaded glass), and Ben Sandoval (woodworking). Abad Lucero returned from Taos to head the furniture production in 1938. Furniture, textiles, and tinwork continued to dominate sales.[43] **E**l Parian Analco closed after the summer of 1938, but The Native Market continued. At the end of 1939 the *Alianza de Artesanos,* or Native Market Guild, a cooperative with twenty-three artisans as charter members, assumed market ownership and management. Remaining merchandise was left on consignment and new objects consigned were similar to those so successfully carried since 1934. However, the loss of Leonora Curtin's subsidy, the availability of federal jobs in programs such as the WPA, and growing uncertainties about war meant that The Alianza Native Market closed in about six months. In many ways this marked the end of the first Hispanic crafts "revival," which William Wroth says began in the early 1920s, peaked in the late 1930s, and died down by World War II:

During this period, in spite of the enthusiasm of the wealthy Anglo patrons in northern New Mexico, Hispanic crafts never "caught on" nationally in the way the Indian crafts did. Interest was fairly well limited to the Southwest and southern California, the areas in which the adobe hacienda revival was taking place. The major interest in Hispanic crafts was as furnishings for these comfortable Southwestern-style adobe homes. These crafts were not, as were the Indian, viewed as valuable art objects in themselves purchased with an eye for speculation.[44]

Brice Sewell, instrumental at the beginning of The Native Market, was also on its committee of nonmember judges in the final six months. The shop had proved a valuable outlet for work by students in the statewide vocational training schools teaching traditional Hispanic crafts that Sewell directed. In 1932 he had been appointed supervisor of trade and industrial education for the New Mexico State Department of Vocational Education (SDVE), with the challenge "to establish in rural communities new vocational schools devoted to the teaching of traditional New Mexican crafts; to develop a meaningful curriculum of the highest quality; and to develop the means of successfully marketing the crafts produced in the schools, so that viable local industries would develop out of the village vocational schools." He hired as staff members woodworker Henry Gonzales, furniture maker Bill Lumpkins, weaver Dolores Perrault Montoya, and teacher Carmen Espinosa, and in 1933 launched what William Wroth calls

an ambitious training program . . . designed to combat the devastating economic effects of drought and depression on the area's Hispanic communities. Vocational schools at Taos and Peñasco in Taos County and at Chupadero, La Cienega, and Galisteo in Santa Fe County were among the earliest established. By utilizing the resources of several state and federal government agencies Sewell was able to expand the program so that by 1936 nearly every Hispanic community of any size had its own vocational school. They ranged from those offering one or two classes in a small rented storefront to full-fledged centers such as the Taos Vocational School with its own adobe building constructed by the local community. . . . [and their] curriculum centered around weaving, tanning and leatherwork, furniture-making and ornamental ironwork.[45]

To help implement this curriculum the SDVE issued and distributed a series of mimeographed *Trade and Industrial Bulletins* edited by Carmen Espinosa during the 1930s. These valuable resources include *Spanish Colonial Furniture Bulletin* (1933, rev. 1935), *New Adaptations from Authentic Examples of Spanish Colonial Furniture* (n.d.), *Vegetable Dyes Bulletin* (1934, rev. October 1935), *New Mexico Colonial Embroidery Bulletin* (1935, rev. July 1943), *Spanish Colonial Painted Chests* (1937), *Weaving Bulletin* (1937), *Graphic Standards for Furniture Designers* (1939), and others on tinwork, tanning, and house construction. **B**rice Sewell's vision for the SDVE training schools also to act as centers for community revitalization in economically strapped areas was born largely of his earlier association with the University of New Mexico's San Jose Experimental School in south Albuquerque. Directed by Dr. Lloyd S. Tireman between 1930 and 1935, it was an elementary school intended to study Hispanic children's educational potential and to train rural schoolteachers. Woodworking, weaving, tanning, tinwork, and Spanish folk songs and folktales were part of the curriculum. Mary Austin was on the school's board of directors and was its "chief publicist," according to Suzanne Forrest:

28. Dolores Perrault (*l.*), Doña Maria Martínez (*c.*), and Atocha Martínez (*r.*) demonstrate wool carding and spinning at the Native Market, Santa Fe, New Mexico. Photo by T. Harmon Parkhurst.
29. The Native Market, Santa Fe, New Mexico. Artist Sheldon Parsons and Dolores Perrault conferring (*front r.*), Doña Maria Martinez spinning and unidentified male weaver working (*l.*), Pedro Quintana in tinwork booth (*r.*), furniture display in rear. **30.** Interior of WPA weaving project shop, September 1939, Costilla, New Mexico. **31.** Couple in their home, January 1943, Peñasco, New Mexico.

[She] . . . summarized the goals of the project as well as its larger vision for New Mexico. Rural New Mexico villages, she wrote, had suffered a total loss of community identity after a half century of indifference and contempt on the part of the dominant Anglo population. All that was dramatic, entertaining, poetic, and generally cultural had dwindled to the vanishing point and village education was completely severed from the community. . . . What rural New Mexicans most needed, she believed, was training in the normal activities of rural community life. The skills of adobe-making, carpentry, weaving, fruit-canning, and bread-making should be taught by selected individuals from the region who would travel from village to village.

17

In 1936 a similar project was set up at the Harwood Foundation in Taos under the direction of J. T. Reid while Tireman went on to direct another at the village of Nambé in 1937. George I. Sanchez, who had worked with Tireman throughout the San Jose project, subsequently conducted a survey of Taos County that was published in 1940 as a landmark book entitled *Forgotten People: A Study of New Mexicans*.[46] The Rio Pueblo District of Taos County, including Peñasco, Chamisal, Vadito, and Rodarte, was earlier surveyed as part of the United States Department of the Interior's Office of Indian Affairs' Indian Land Research Unit's three-volume *Tewa Basin Study* of 1935. Volume 2, "The Spanish-American Villages," covered more than thirty communities from Nambe and Pojoaque to Truchas, Las Trampas, Abiquiú, and El Rito. Besides those in SDVE programs, craftspeople were noted among the "about 20,000 Spanish-Americans in the area, . . . [who] make up between 80 and 90 percent of the whole population." Weavers were reported in Nambe, San Ildefonso, Puebla, Cuarteles, Cundiyo, Córdova, Truchas, Angostura, Barranca, Chamita, Ojo Sarco, Las Trampas, the Rio Pueblo District, and Chimayó, which boasted ninety to a hundred weavers and six blanket dealers. Two wood-carvers were found: "one fair wood-carver who averages some $15 per month on the sale of his work" in Las Trampas and José Dolores López in Córdova, who is unnamed:

The best money in the village is made by a woodcarver, whose work has become quite famous. This man is working on an art basis, however, and is undoubtedly somewhat of a genius in his line.

A blacksmith was discovered in Angostura and a silverworker who was also a weaver in Barranca.[47] Traditional arts and building skills were also documented by photographers working for the Farm Security Administration (FSA). First established on April 30, 1935, as the Resettlement Administration, it was an independent agency to provide short-term relief for impoverished farm families and long-term rural rebuilding. In 1937 it became part of the U.S. Department of Agriculture and changed its name. Roy Emerson Stryker headed the agency's Historical Section with a broad mandate to direct investigators, photographers, economists, sociologists, and statisticians. He set up an Information Division to provide unified photographic services and eventually employed photographers Arthur Rothstein, Carl Mydans, Walker Evans, Ben Shahn, Dorothea Lange, Paul Carter, Theodor Jung, Russell Lee, John Vachon, Marion Post Wolcott, Jack Delano, and John Collier, Jr. Several did photodocumentary work in New Mexico, including significant Hispanic village studies by Russell Lee and John Collier, Jr.[48] Extreme poverty characterized most FSA photodocumentary subjects, as it had in the *Tewa Basin Study* area, where many men were noted as working for the Civilian Conservation Corps or the Federal Emergency Relief Administration. The study was completed shortly after President Franklin D. Roosevelt addressed the Congress on January 3, 1935, and declared: "The Federal Government

must and shall quit this business of relief. . . .We must preserve not only the bodies of the unemployed from destitution, but also their self-respect, their self-reliance, and courage and determination." He signed Executive Order No. 7034 on May 6, thereby establishing the Works Progress Administration (WPA) to coordinate "the work relief program as a whole" and to "recommend and carry on small useful projects designed to assure a maximum employment in all localities." In New Mexico, where the WPA soon became known popularly as *"El Diablo a pie,"* the Devil on foot, a jocular hispanicization of its initials' English pronunciation, Roswell's Lea Rowland was appointed state administrator.[49] White-collar jobs were to be included in the WPA, and on August 2, 1935, Federal Project Number One was announced:

It is the intention of this Administration to sponsor nation-wide projects intending to employ persons now on relief who are qualified in fields of Art, Music, Drama, and Writing. The following persons have been appointed by [WPA Federal Administrator] Mr. [Harry] Hopkins to direct each of these nation-wide projects: Art, Holger Cahill; Music, Nikolai Sokoloff; Drama, Hallie Flanagan; and Writers, Henry G. Alsberg.

Thus began what historian William F. McDonald calls the "heart" of a government-supported and -subsidized arts program that "in material size and cultural character was unprecedented in the history of this or any other nation."[50] Russell Vernon Hunter directed the New Mexico Federal Art Project (NMFAP) when it began, Helen Chandler Ryan directed the New Mexico Federal Music Project (NMFMP), and Ina Sizer Cassidy directed the New Mexico Federal Writers' Project (NMFWP). The Federal Art Project (FAP) had been preceded by the Public Works of Art Project (PWAP), established by a grant from the Civil Works Administration to the Treasury Department in December 1933. New Mexico was with Arizona in Region 13, directed by Jesse Nusbaum. Gustave Baumann coordinated work within the state. Córdova's José Dolores López is listed as a PWAP artist in Baumann's 1934 report.[51] With Arizona, Colorado, Utah, and Wyoming, New Mexico was in FAP Region Five, headed by Donald Bear. Russell Vernon directed the NMFAP from its inception in October 1935 until its close late in 1942. He was assisted by Joy Yeck, and his first state advisory committee included Paul A. F. Walter (President, First National Bank, Santa Fe), Mary R. Van Stone (Curator, Museum of New Mexico Fine Arts Museum), Francis del Dosso (art instructor at the University of New Mexico), and artists Raymond Jonson, Gustave Baumann, and Randall Davey. The NMFAP was considered exemplary, employing 206 persons between 1935 and 1939. Art teaching and exhibition centers were established at Melrose, Roswell, Las Vegas, and Gallup.[52] William Wroth calls the NMFAP "a small program focussed upon quality." Painter Russell Vernon Hunter, who once worked for Brice Sewell in the SDVE, was able with help from Leonora Curtin to convince FAP director Holger Cahill that Hispanic arts were aesthet-

32. Main altar of church at Las Trampas, New Mexico, January 1943. Photographer of this image, John Collier, Jr., wrote: "All within the church are common property and an individual or group can carry a santo home for the night returning it the next morning. These four men are borrowing santos for their chapel, three miles over the mountains."

33. Side altar of Las Trampas church, January 1943. Photographer of this image, John Collier, Jr., wrote: "The prevailing colors are grey and blue. A Coca-Cola bottle is used as a candle holder."

ically and culturally important. FAP workers decorated many public buildings in the Spanish Colonial style. Notable in this regard is the Albuquerque Little Theatre, designed by John Gaw Meem and opened in 1936. Hispanic artisans who helped with its interior decoration include tinworker Eddie Delgado, wood-carver Patrocinio Barela, *colcha* embroiderer Stella Garcia, and woodworker George Segura. Among Hunter's personal "discoveries" were self-taught artist Patrocinio Barela of Taos, carver Juan Sanchez of Colmor, painter Pedro Cervantes of Texico, and straw appliqué worker Ernesto Roybal of Española. Hunter also instigated the *Portfolio of Spanish Colonial Design* project directed by E. Boyd Hall and completed by August 1, 1938.[53] Like Hunter, Helen Chandler Ryan of Albuquerque served as director of her Federal One Project throughout its existence. She was appointed to head the New Mexico Federal Music Project (NMFMP) on January 1, 1936. Groups playing Hispanic music under NMFMP auspices included the Children's Tipica Orchestra of Albuquerque led

by Pedro Valles, a Tipica Orchestra directed by Pablo Mares in Las Vegas, and the Hernández brothers' guitar ensemble from Bernalillo. In 1938 NMFMP teachers directed children performing *Los Pastores* in the Palace of the Governors. Ryan encouraged the collection of Hispanic folk songs by the University of New Mexico's Arthur L. Campa and Aureliano Armendáriz of La Mesilla. Among the mimeographed collections published were "Spanish-American Folk Songs of New Mexico" (1936–37), "Guitar method with guitar arrangements of Spanish-American folk songs of New Mexico" (1939), "Spanish-American Singing Games of New Mexico" (1940, subsequently incorporated into *The Spanish-American Song and Game Book,* published by A. S. Barnes of New York in 1942), and "Spanish-American Dance Tunes of New Mexico" (1942).[54] Three directors headed the New Mexico Federal Writers' Project (later Writers' Program): Ina Sizer Cassidy from October 1, 1935, until January 1939; Aileen Nusbaum from February 1 through August 31, 1939; and

Charles Ethrige Minton from then until the program's end in 1942. Many of the field writers were Hispanic and/or submitted material on Hispanic folkways. Notable contributions came from Lorin W. Brown of Santa Fe, and Córdova, Reyes N. Martínez of Arroyo Hondo, Aurora Lucero White of Las Vegas, Annette Hesch Thorp of Santa Fe, and Bright Lynn of Las Vegas.[55] Some of this material was published in a mimeographed periodical, *Over the Turquoise Trail,* in 1937. The major work of the Federal Writers' Project was the production of the American Guide Series, an enterprise that underwent many changes. Alice Corbin Henderson served as editor for New Mexico's guide between February 1936 and July 1937 and complained to Cassidy in a 1936 letter about the difficulties of her task with too few personnel "and, in spite of all the books . . . written about New Mexico, mostly the northern part, . . . great areas practically untouched." A state handbook of 1938 proclaimed: "This Guide will be vastly more elaborate and detailed than any guide hitherto published by a firm or City. No section of the State is to be neglected by the Guide." Idaho writer Vardis Fisher came to Santa Fe in 1939 to help develop a compelling style for presenting the guide, since Washington, D.C., officials wanted "the type of visual description that Steinbeck would give—that is, descriptions of the types of buildings common to smaller New Mexican towns, mention of color, smells, sounds, signs, and above all, of the types of people seen along the streets." In the end, New Mexico's contribution to the American Guide Series was late. Selling for $2.50 and published by the New York firm of Hastings House in August 1940, *New Mexico: A Guide to the Colorful State* never reached the state until September of that year, too late for most of the summertime Coronado Cuarto Centennial activities.[56] Impetus for the Coronado Cuarto Centennial came from Roswell schoolteacher Charles M. Martin, whose idea in 1930 to give national currency to New Mexico history was "just one of those inspirations a man is glad to have to give to his state." He took a resolution to the Roswell chapter of the New Mexico Archaeological and Historical Society on February 19, 1931, declaring: "Other states have held elaborate ceremonies at their Hundredth Anniversaries. We are entitled to hold an even greater celebration at our Four Hundredth Anniversary." In 1935 Gov. Clyde Tingley signed a legislative act creating the Coronado Cuarto Centennial Commission with University of New Mexico president Dr. James F. Zimmerman as president, Albuquerque writer Erna Fergusson as vice president, Albuquerque lawyer Gilberto Espinosa as secretary, and Santa Fe businessman Henry Dendahl as treasurer. By adding Arizona, Texas, Colorado, Kansas, and Oklahoma to the plans, they were able to obtain two hundred thousand dollars in federal funds in 1939, when a United States Coronado Exposition Committee was established. It included Vice President John N. Garner, Speaker of the House of Representatives William H. Bankhead, Secretary of the Interior Harold L. Ickes, Secretary of Commerce Harry L. Hopkins, and Clinton P. Anderson as managing director. In 1940 the New Mexico Coronado

Cuarto Centennial Commission comprised Dr. James F. Zimmerman (president), Erna Fergusson (vice president), Gilberto Espinosa (secretary-treasurer), Riley M. Edwards, Ruth Laughlin Alexander, Concha Ortiz y Pino, Charles L. Martin, Orval Ricketts, B. C. Hernandez, and, ex officio, Joseph A. Bursey, Director New Mexico State Tourist Bureau.[57] In 1938 University of New Mexico president James F. Zimmerman proclaimed:

With the celebration of her four hundredth birthday, New Mexico will have an unprecedented opportunity to further the cultural relations between the United States of America and those countries lying to the South, whose historic background is so linked with ours. To this day a large portion of New Mexico is Spanish in blood and thinking. Through the Coronado celebration, we shall unite our colorful past with the realities of the present, and in so doing lay new foundations of spiritual relationship with our sister nations in this hemisphere.[58]

His rhetoric is reminiscent of that implicit in House Bill 164 of March 1925, which authorized the new state flag designed by public health officer and amateur archaeologist Dr. Harry P. Mera: "Said flag shall be the ancient Zia Sun Symbol of red in the center of a field of yellow. The colors shall be the red and yellow of old Spain." The official flag salute calls it "the Zia symbol of perfect friendship among united cultures."[59] Erna Fergusson explained the genesis of the Coronado *Entradas* (Entrances) as vehicles "to make the uninformed aware of Coronado and of his importance, . . . to attract people to New Mexico, [and] to present the story as a living thing, some sort of dramatic presentation." Thomas Wood Stevens, who had worked with the de Vargas *Entrada* in the 1920s Santa Fe fiestas, "acknowledged master of pageantry, wrote the script which is presented by a cast of hundreds, many mounted, all costumed, armored, and accoutred with absolute historic accuracy." Fundamentally, however, the Coronado festivities were economically motivated, in many respects the automobile's equivalent to the earlier Great Southwest of the Santa Fe Railway and the Fred Harvey Company. A 1938 booklet, *What the Coronado Cuarto Centennial Means to New Mexico,* claims: "If our many local celebrations are responsible for one car out of twenty remaining in the state one extra day, then the total increase in income from tourists should be between SEVEN AND EIGHT MILLION DOLLARS." In the June 1940 Coronado issue of *New Mexico Magazine* Edmund Sherman announced:

Colorful New Mexico will be more colorful than ever. To the regular summer events and celebrations that attract visitors from throughout the world will be added the Entradas *and the nearly two hundred folk festivals scattered throughout the State all during the summer. . . . Virtually every activity of the summer, regular or special, will have some sort of tie-up with the Coronado celebration, whether it's conventions, coiffures, costumes, styles, sports, foods. Even tourists crossing the State in a few hours can hardly miss contact some way or other with the 400th anniversary celebration.[60]*

It was fitting, therefore, that the Coronado Cuarto Centennial

34. Title page, *Portfolio of Spanish Colonial Design in New Mexico,* WPA New Mexico Federal Art Project, August 1, 1938. **35.** Hand-colored rendering of St. Acathius (*San Acacio*) santo, *Portfolio of Spanish Colonial Design,* 1938. **36.** Hand-colored rendering of St. James, Moorslayer (*Santiago*), *colcha, Portfolio of Spanish Colonial Design,* 1938. **37.** Store window displaying Coronado Cuarto Centennial souvenirs and publications, 1940, Santa Fe, New Mexico.

38. *Entrada*, Coronado Cuarto Centennial, 1940, Santa Fe, New Mexico.

Commission joined the University of New Mexico in sponsoring the WPA Writers' Program's *New Mexico: A Guide to the Colorful State* since most of its 496 pages contain 25 automobile tours covering almost every community in the state. Among the sixteen introductory essays is one on "New Mexican Art," with a section about "Spanish Colonial Art." Frank Applegate, Mary Austin, the Spanish Colonial Arts Society, and the SDVE are cited in this section, which concludes:

Through the arts of the native people, the contemporary artists who visited New Mexico found a deeper fulfillment than is afforded by mere 'picturesqueness.' During a time when it was proper to go to Europe for traditional background, they stumbled upon sources which made them feel at home in North America, the sources existing in the Spanish-Americans. It gave to those modern explorers a sense of art heritage which they could not find in any other place in their homeland.[61]

This is the sort of sentiment that prompted Edgar Lee Hewett to observe in his introduction to the special Coronado Cuarto Centennial issue of the *Santa Fe New Mexican* on June 26, 1940:

The arts have kept Santa Fe from becoming an "up-to-date burg" and made it unique and beautiful among the capitals of our country. In the monolithic Palace of the Governors, the Art Gallery, La Fonda, in many public buildings, business houses, and in countless residences, the fine old architectural tradition of the region has been preserved and population and values have increased amazingly. Santa Fe doesn't advertise for tourists or residents. They can't be kept away. Artists and writers constitute only a small percentage of the population, but their influence is wherever you look.

NOTES

1. Edgar Lee Hewett, "Introduction" to "Artists and Writers: A List of Prominent Artists and Writers of New Mexico," 26 June 1940 special issue of the *Santa Fe New Mexican* reprinted as part of Marta Weigle and Kyle Fiore, eds., *New Mexico Artists and Writers: A Celebration, 1940* (Santa Fe: Ancient City Press, 1982), 3.

2. Carl D. Sheppard, *Creator of the Santa Fe Style: Isaac Hamilton Rapp, Architect* (Albuquerque: University of New Mexico Press with Historical Society of New Mexico, 1988), 74–75, 77; photo of Colorado Supply Company warehouse, 59. On Curtiss see Virginia L. Grattan, *Mary Colter: Builder Upon the Red Earth* (Flagstaff, Ariz.: Northland Press, 1980), 22. Also see Nicholas C. Markovich, "Santa Fe Renaissance: City Planning and Stylistic Preservation, 1912," in Markovich, Wolfgang F. E. Preiser, and Fred G. Sturm, eds., *Pueblo Style and Regional Architecture* (New York: Van Nostrand Reinhold, 1992), 197–212.
Contemporary Santa Fe style was canonized and widely popularized by Christine Mather, Curator of Spanish Colonial Collections at the Museum of International Folk Art, Santa Fe, and Sharon Woods in their full-color, 264-page

Santa Fe Style (New York: Rizzoli International Publications, 1986). Also see Marta Weigle, "Southwest Lures: Innocents Detoured, Incensed Determined," *Journal of the Southwest* 32 (1990): 499–540; Weigle, "Selling the Southwest: Santa Fe InSites," in Scott Norris, ed., *Discovered Country: Tourism and Survival in the American West* (Albuquerque: Stone Ladder Press, 1994), 210–24.

3. Christopher Wilson, "The Spanish Pueblo Revival Defined, 1904–1921," *New Mexico Studies in the Fine Arts* 7 (1982): 24–30. This material is based on chapter 4, "Creating the Tourist Plaza: 1880–1921," of "The Santa Fe, New Mexico Plaza: An Architectural and Cultural History, 1610–1921" (M.A. thesis, University of New Mexico, December 1981), 105–58. Also see Chris Wilson, "New Mexico in the Tradition of Romantic Reaction," in Markovich et al., *Pueblo Style*, 175–94.

4. James T. Stensvaag, "Clio on the Frontier: The Intellectual Evolution of the Historical Society of New Mexico, 1859–1925," *New Mexico Historical Review* 55 (1980): 301–3; Marta Weigle, "The First Twenty-Five Years of the Spanish Colonial Arts Society," in Weigle with Claudia Larcombe and Samuel Larcombe, eds., *Hispanic Arts and Ethnohistory in the Southwest:*

New Papers Inspired by the Work of E. Boyd (Santa Fe: Ancient City Press; Albuquerque: University of New Mexico Press, 1983), 182.

5. E. Boyd, *Popular Arts of Spanish New Mexico* (Santa Fe: Museum of New Mexico Press, 1974), 38; Wilson, "Spanish Pueblo Revival," 27.

6. Sylvanus Griswold Morley, "Santa Fe Architecture," *Old Santa Fe* 2, 3 (January 1915): 282, 283–84, 300, 292.

7. Wilson, "Spanish Pueblo Revival," 29; Carlos Vierra, "New Mexico Architecture," *Art and Archaeology* 7, 1/2 (January/February 1918): 37–49; "Museum and School Share in San Diego's Triumph," *El Palacio* 2, 2 (November 1914): 2. The murals are illustrated in Paul A. F. Walter, "New Mexico's Contribution to the Panama–California Exposition," *El Palacio* 3, 1 (October 1915): 3–16. On the California Building see Florence Christman, *The Romance of Balboa Park*, 4th ed. rev. (San Diego: San Diego Historical Society, 1985), 57–60.

8. Carl Sheppard, *The Saint Francis Murals of Santa Fe: The Commission and the Artists* (Santa Fe: Sunstone Press, 1989), 93.

9. Robert W. Rydell, *All the World's a Fair: Visions of Empire at American International Expositions, 1876–1916* (Chicago: University of Chicago Press, 1984), 209, 217, 219–20; Christman, *Balboa Park*, 60. Also see David Gebhard, "The Myth and Power of Place: Hispanic Revivalism in the American Southwest," in Markovich et al., *Pueblo Style*, 143–58.

10. Michael Miller, "New Mexico's Role in the Panama–California Exposition of 1915," *El Palacio* 91, 2 (Fall 1985): 13–17; *New Mexico The Land of Opportunity: Official Data on the Resources and Industries of New Mexico—The Sunshine State* (Albuquerque: Press of the *Albuquerque Morning Journal*, 1915). Edited by Commissioner of Publicity A. E. Koehler, Jr., this "official souvenir" contains short essays on many aspects of the new state's history and commerce together with brief county and city histories and descriptions.

11. Sheppard, *Creator of the Santa Fe Style*, 46, 79–88; Wilson, "Spanish Pueblo Revival," 28. San Diego's New Mexico Building has been much remodeled and is now the Balboa Park Club (Christman, *Balboa Park*, 61).

12. Marta Weigle and Kyle Fiore, *Santa Fe and Taos: The Writer's Era, 1916–1941* (Santa Fe: Ancient City Press, 1982), 9–10; Wilson, "Spanish Pueblo Revival," 30.

13. Ruth Laughlin Barker, "Keeping the Oldest Capital Old," *Sunset* 37 (September 1916): 34.

14. "The Santa Fe Fiesta," *El Palacio* 7 (1919): 99–101.

15. Thomas E. Chávez, "Santa Fe's Own: A History of Fiesta," *El Palacio* 91, 1 (Spring 1985): 11–13. Also see Ronald L. Grimes, *Symbol and Conquest: Public Ritual and Drama in Santa Fe, New Mexico* (Ithaca, N.Y.: Cornell University Press, 1976), 186–87; Wayne Mauzy, "The Tertio-Millennial Exposition," *El Palacio* 37, 24–25–26 (December 12–19–26, 1934): 185–99.

16. "The 1925 Santa Fe Fiesta," *El Palacio* 18 (1925): 88–91; *Papers of the School of American Research: The Fiesta Book* (Santa Fe: Archaeological Institute of America, 1925); Grimes, *Symbol and Conquest,* 187–88. For more on Thomas Wood Stevens see David Glassberg, *American Pageantry: The Uses of Tradition in the Early Twentieth Century* (Chapel Hill: University of North Carolina Press, 1990).

17. See, e.g., James Marshall, *Santa Fe: The Railroad That Built an Empire* (New York: Random House, 1945); Keith L. Bryant, Jr., *History of the Atchison, Topeka and Santa Fe Railway* (New York: Macmillan, 1974); James David Henderson, *"Meals by Fred Harvey": A Phenomenon of the American West* (Fort Worth: Texas Christian University Press, 1968). On the predominantly natural wonderland and Native American advertising campaigns see T. C. McLuhan, *Dream Tracks: The Railroad and the American Indian, 1890–1930,* with photographs from the William E. Kopplin Collection (New York: Harry N. Abrams, 1985); Marta Weigle, "From Desert to Disney World: The Santa Fe Railway and the Fred Harvey Company Display the Indian Southwest," *Journal of Anthropological Research* 45 (1989): 115–37; Sandra D'Emilio and Suzan Campbell, *Visions and Visionaries: The Art and Artists of the Santa Fe Railway* (Salt Lake City: Peregrine Smith Books, 1991); Weigle, "Exposition and Mediation: Mary Colter, Erna Fergusson, and the Santa Fe/Harvey Popularization of the Native Southwest, 1902–1940," *Frontiers: A Journal of Women Studies* 12, 3 (1992): 117–50.

18. Robert E. Pounds, *Santa Fe Depots—The Western Lines* (Dallas: Kachina Press, 1984), 17, 22, 24, 57; Louise Ivers, "The Architecture of Las Vegas, New Mexico" (Ph.D. diss., University of New Mexico, 1975), 215–20. On architect Roehrig see, e.g., Karen J. Weitze, *California's Mission Revival* (Los Angeles: Hennessey & Ingalls, 1984), 60, 64, 66, 68, 74–75, 139.

19. Pounds, *Santa Fe Depots,* 60, 64; Weitze, *Mission Revival,* 92; Marc Simmons, *Albuquerque: A Narrative History* (Albuquerque: University of New Mexico Press, 1982), 329. Also see David Gebhard, "Architecture and the Fred Harvey Houses: The Alvarado and La Fonda," *New Mexico Architecture* (January–February 1964): 18–25; "The Alvarado Hotel," *New Mexico Architecture* (November-December 1969): 20–22; John P. Conron, "The Alvarado Hotel,"

New Mexico Architecture (May-June 1970): 16–19. The Alvarado was closed on January 2, 1970; wrecking crews dismantled and demolished it in February and March of that year.

20. Wilson, "The Santa Fe Plaza," 109. George Hickox took part of his filigree workshop to the Cincinnati Exposition in 1884. An eastern newspaper described how "a couple of his native workmen, bronze tinted young fellows, who sit behind their benches, and with an air of general melachoy [sic] create, with the assistance of the spirit lamp, out of silver threads marvelous fruit and flowers of gold and silver, such as we read of in the *Arabian Nights*. . .To see the dusky face of the workman bending over the blow pipe, welding the tiny bits together, and their looking at the completed work, fragile and light as thistle down, we fancied a breath can destroy it as a breath had made it" (ibid., 110).
William Wroth notes the intensified, late nineteenth-century demand for filigree jewelry and the large number of such artists in Santa Fe, but he claims that "filigree work continued to have some vogue in New Mexico until World War II when the interest died off and was replaced by the growing demand for Indian jewelry" ("Jewelry in Spanish New Mexico: Some Thoughts on the Arts of the *Platero*," in Wroth, ed., *Hispanic Crafts of the Southwest* [Colorado Springs: Taylor Museum of the Colorado Springs Fine Arts Center, 1977], 67).

21. Bart Ripp, "Jewels from the desert: Fred Harvey man fathered modern Indian arts, crafts," *Albuquerque Tribune,* 23 November 1987, B-1, B-8; Boyd, *Popular Arts,* 432. For notes on some of Schweizer's Mexican trips see Bertha P. Dutton, "Commerce on a New Frontier: The Fred Harvey Company and the Fred Harvey Fine Arts Collection," in Christine Mather, ed., *Colonial Frontiers: Art and Life in Spanish New Mexico, The Fred Harvey Collection* (Santa Fe: Ancient City Press, 1983), 95–98.

22. Janet Smith, "Notable Collections: The Fred Harvey Collection of Santos, at Albuquerque," 1,200 words, 5 pp., 20 April 1936 (WPA Files, New Mexico State Records Center and Archives [NMSRC], Santa Fe, folder no. 528).

23. Janet Smith, "Interesting Collections: The Fred Harvey Indian Building," 800 words, 4 pp., n.d. (WPA Files, NMSRC, no. 143); Barbara A. Babcock, Guy and Doris Monthan, *The Pueblo Storyteller: Development of a Figurative Ceramic Tradition* (Tucson: University of Arizona Press, 1986), 11, 14, 17; Wilson, "The Santa Fe Plaza," 109, 117, photo 238.
Sarah Nestor gives a different account of Gold: "The most famous store was the Candelario's Original Old Curio Store on San Francisco Street in Santa Fe, which had its origins in a general store and meat market owned by the Spanish New Mexican family in the late nineteenth century. The Candelario brothers appointed Jake Gold, 'the forerunner of all curio dealers,' as its manager in the 1880s. Gold added crafts and curios to the general merchandise, and named the store the Original Jake Gold Curio Store. The Candelarios later named the store The Original Old Curio Store and dispensed with Gold's

services in 1903, but they continued to barter supplies for New Mexico Indian and Spanish crafts. Families who came from rural areas to barter were housed and fed in the Candelario Compound adjoining the store, their burros lodged in a nearby yard in Burro Alley. As business expanded the store's goods were increased by the hiring of Indian, Spanish, and Mexican craftsmen to work on the spot. The Original Old Curio Store was the most fabulous store in the Southwest in its day, housing a vast array of junk and treasures" (*The Native Market of the Spanish New Mexican Craftsmen: Santa Fe, 1933–1940* [Santa Fe: Colonial New Mexico Historical Foundation, 1978], 3–4).

24. Pounds, *Santa Fe Depots,* 56, 60; David Gebhard, "Architecture and the Fred Harvey Houses," *New Mexico Architecture* (July/August 1962): 16; Grattan, *Mary Colter,* 22, 25, photos 23, 24. Sylvanus Griswold Morley commends "the quaint script of 'El Ortiz' above the main entrance" and notes: "The name El Ortiz was suggested by Col. R. E. Twitchell, and is an abbreviation for Nicolas Ortiz Nino Ledrom de Guevaca, one of the reconquistadores under Diego de Vargas" ("Development of the Santa Fe Style of Architecture," *The Santa Fe Magazine, Railway Exchange, Chicago* 9, 7 [June 1915]: 30).

25. Sheppard, *Creator of Santa Fe Style,* 94–95; Bainbridge Bunting, *John Gaw Meem: Southwestern Architect* (Albuquerque: University of New Mexico Press, School of American Research Book, 1983), 74.

26. *La Fonda in Old Santa Fé: The Inn at the End of the Trail* (Chicago: Rand McNally, July 1929), 2; Grattan, *Mary Colter,* 52.

27. *Indian-detours: Most distinctive Motor Cruise service in the world* (Chicago: Rand McNally, 1930), 10. William E. Tydeman has studied the collection of lantern slides from these lectures, during which, "from 1926 to 1941, in a remarkable record of endurance, Elizabeth De Huff offered tourists a perception of the cultures of the Southwest." The slides focus on the pueblos; the collection "contains not a single slide of a Hispanic. However, to promote effectively the fifty miles surrounding Santa Fe, other Hispanic images had to be included: churches, archaeological sites, and homes festooned with chili peppers and ristras [strands of chile peppers]. There were photographs of wood wagons and the standard imagery of the wood-bearing burro, but never—except for one image of Penitentes carrying a cross—a Hispanic face. While this avoidance of Hispanic people may be surprising it is not exceptional. The same stereotyping and racism are found in the conventional written sources of the period" ("New Mexico Tourist Images," in Judith Boyce DeMark, ed., *Essays in Twentieth-Century New Mexico History* [Albuquerque: University of New Mexico Press, 1994], 203–4, 206).

28. *Indian-detours,* 1; D. H. Thomas, *The Southwestern Indian Detours: The Story of the Fred Harvey/Santa Fe Railway Experiment in "Detourism"* (Phoenix: Hunter Publishing, 1978), 122. Tydeman argues that Indian Detours generally

chose "to emphasize the architectural and mission tradition of New Mexico life, to promote a celebration of the ties to the grand tradition of Spain, but to avoid any reference to New Mexico Hispanics or village life [because] the racism and class consciousness of eastern tourists made it hard to turn New Mexico's Hispanic life into a commodity" ("Tourist Images," 205).

29. Charles L. Briggs, "The Role of *Mexicano* Artists and the Anglo Elite in the Emergence of a Contemporary Folk Art," in John Michael Vlach and Simon J. Bronner, eds., *Folk Art and Art Worlds,* (1986; new edition, Logan: Utah State University Press, 1992), 208, 211. Lorin W. Brown recalls his Córdova visitors to Lorenzo de Córdova [pseud.], *Echoes of the Flute* (Santa Fe: Ancient City Press, 1972), 9–11. Elsewhere, Brown describes Córdova's deformed idiot or *inocente* Onésimo, who "was a great handshaker. . .[and] appointed himself official greeter for all newcomers or visitors to the village. Being from a village which attracted many tourists, Onésimo was kept busy greeting them whether they liked it or not. No sooner did a Harvey car or any other vehicle stop and its passengers start to alight than Onésimo would advance in his usual form, left hand aiding his suspenders and right hand extended in greeting. Many were the involuntary shrieks and shrinking retreats, but Onésimo insisted on shaking hands with each and every one" (Lorin W. Brown with Charles L. Briggs and Marta Weigle, *Hispano Folklife of New Mexico: The Lorin W. Brown Federal Writers' Project Manuscripts* [Albuquerque: University of New Mexico Press, 1978], 121).

30. *They Know New Mexico: Intimate Sketches by Western Writers* (Passenger Department, AT&SF Railway, 1928), 39.

31. Alice Corbin, "Furniture for Spanish Colonial Homes," *House and Garden,* (July 1928): 62, 92, 106, as cited in Lonn Taylor and Dessa Bokides, *New Mexican Furniture, 1600–1940: The Origins, Survival, and Revival of Furniture Making in the Hispanic Southwest* (Santa Fe: Museum of New Mexico Press, 1987), 219.

32. *They Know New Mexico,* 13–14.

33. Alice Corbin Henderson, *Brothers of Light: The Penitentes of the Southwest* (New York: Harcourt, Brace, 1937), 37, 55.

34. Suzanne Forrest, *The Preservation of the Village: New Mexico's Hispanics and the New Deal* (Albuquerque: University of New Mexico Press, 1989), 47–48, 62; Roland F. Dickey, *New Mexico Village Arts* (1949; reprint, Albuquerque: University of New Mexico Press, 1970), 241.

35. Nina Otero-Warren, *Old Spain in Our Southwest* (New York: Harcourt, Brace, 1936); Charlotte Whaley, *Nina Otero-Warren of Santa Fe* (Albuquerque: University of New Mexico Press, 1994); Cleofas M. Jaramillo, *Shadows of the Past (Sombras del pasado)* (Santa Fe: Seton Village Press, 1941), 10.

36. Genaro M. Padilla, *My History, Not Yours: The Formation of Mexican American Autobiography*

(Madison: University of Wisconsin Press, 1993), 223. Padilla cites page numbers in Cleofas M. Jaramillo, *Romance of a Little Village Girl* (San Antonio: Naylor, 1955). Also see Tey Diana Rebolledo, "*Las Escritoras*: Romances and Realities," in Erlinda Gonzales-Berry, ed. *Pasó por Aquí: Critical Essays on the New Mexican Literary Tradition, 1542–1988* (Albuquerque: University of New Mexico Press, 1989), 199–214.

37. Briggs, "*Mexicano* Artists and Anglo Elite," 207–8, 217, 218. Sarah Deutsch sees a similar dilemma in the New Deal cultural revival programs: "By channeling relief funds for Hispanic areas into such projects as Spanish colonial crafts training, governmental programs encouraged cultural isolation, whether or not they intended it. Anti-modernist Anglos, grappling with real problems of geographic isolation and poverty in the villages, saw in colonial cultural revival the economic salvation of the Hispanic villages, and the spiritual salvation of modern America. But however beneficent their impulse, they often did not understand Hispanic villagers' mores and desires, and their movement had other implications" (*No Separate Refuge: Culture, Class, and Gender on an Anglo-Hispanic Frontier in the American Southwest, 1880–1940* [New York: Oxford University Press, 1987], 208).

38. Weigle, "First Twenty-Five Years of SCAS," 190; *La Fonda in Old Santa Fé*, 3; Nestor, *Native Market*, 4–5. Nestor says that Yontz opened in 1902, Gans in 1915, the others in the 1920s.

39. Nestor, ibid., 18, 20–21.

40. Ibid., 21, 23, 31–32.

41. William Wroth, "The Hispanic Craft Revival in New Mexico," in Janet Kardon, ed., *Revivals! Diverse Traditions, 1920–1945: The History of Twentieth-Century American Craft* (New York: Harry N. Abrams with the American Craft Museum, 1994), 90.

42. Nestor, *Native Market*, 35–46.

43. Ibid., 47, 49.

44. Ibid., 51–53; William Wroth, "Introduction: Hispanic Southwestern Craft Traditions in

the 20th Century," in his *Hispanic Crafts of the Southwest*, 6.

45. William Wroth, "New Hope in Hard Times: Hispanic Crafts are Revived During Troubled Years," *El Palacio* 89, 2 (Summer 1983): 26; Nestor, *Native Market*, 12–18; Wroth, preface (identical in both) to his edited publications of the SDVE Bulletins: *Furniture from the Hispanic Southwest: Authentic Designs* (Santa Fe: Ancient City Press, 1984) and *Weaving and Colcha from the Hispanic Southwest* (Santa Fe: Ancient City Press, 1985).

46. Forrest, *Preservation of the Village*, 72–74; George I. Sánchez, *Forgotten People: A Study of New Mexicans* (Albuquerque: University of New Mexico Press, 1940).

47. Marta Weigle, ed., *Hispanic Villages of Northern New Mexico: A Reprint of Volume II of The 1935 Tewa Basin Study, with Supplementary Materials* (Santa Fe: Lightning Tree, Jene Lyon, Publisher, 1975), 33. Data on crafts comes from the reprint of vol. 2 in this edition: weaving, 41, 57, 81, 82, 101, 106, 112, 131, 159, 168, 199, 204, 210; Chimayó, 90–91; Las Trampas wood-carver, 204; Cordova wood-carver, 106–107; blacksmith, 131; silverworker, 159.

48. William Wroth, ed., *Russell Lee's FSA Photographs of Chamisal and Peñasco, New Mexico* (Santa Fe: Ancient City Press; Colorado Springs, Colorado: Taylor Museum of the Colorado Springs Fine Arts Center, 1985); Nancy Wood, *Heartland New Mexico: Photographs from the Farm Security Administration, 1935–1943* (Albuquerque: University of New Mexico Press, 1989); *Far from Main Street: Three Photographers in Depression-Era New Mexico, Russell Lee, John Collier, Jr., and Jack Delano* (Santa Fe: Museum of New Mexico Press, 1994). For an overview of the FSA see F. Jack Hurley, *Portrait of a Decade: Roy Stryker and the Development of Documentary Photography in the Thirties* (Baton Rouge: Louisiana State University Press, 1972); Roy E. Stryker and Nancy Wood, *In This Proud Land: America 1935–1943 as Seen in the FSA Photographs* (Greenwich, Conn.: New York Graphic Society, 1973); Carl Fleischhauer and Beverly W. Bannan, eds., *Documenting America, 1935–1943* (Berkeley:

University of California Press in association with the Library of Congress, 1988).

49. William F. McDonald, *Federal Relief Administration and the Arts* (Columbus: Ohio State University Press, 1969), 103; Marta Weigle, "Appendix: Notes on Federal Project One and the Federal Writers' Project in New Mexico," in Brown with Briggs and Weigle, *Hispano Folklife of New Mexico*, 240.

50. McDonald, *Federal Relief Administration*, 104, 129. A fifth sub-project of Federal One, the Historical Records Survey directed by Luther H. Evans, was not established until November 16, 1935. Note that, effective July 1, 1939, the Works Progress Administration became the Work Projects Administration. Federal One was discontinued as of August 31, with control of the reorganized and diminished projects returned to the states. They were renamed the Art Program, the Music Program, and the Writers' Program.

51. Marta Weigle, ed., *New Mexicans in Cameo and Camera: New Deal Documentation of Twentieth-Century Lives* (Albuquerque: University of New Mexico Press, 1985), 215–16.

52. Ibid., 214. For an overview of the FAP see McDonald, *Federal Relief Administration*, 341–482; Richard D. McKinzie, *The New Deal for Artists* (Princeton: Princeton University Press, 1973), 75–171; Francis V. O'Connor, ed., *Art for the Millions: Essays from the 1930s by Artists and Administrators of the WPA Federal Art Project* (Boston: New York Graphic Society, 1973).

53. Wroth, "Hispanic Craft Revival," 90–93. Also see chapter 2.

54. Charles R. Cutter, "The WPA Federal Music Project in New Mexico," *New Mexico Historical Review* 61 (1986): 207, 208, 211–12; Weigle, "Notes on Federal One," 242, 251–52. For an overview of the FMP see McDonald, *Federal Relief Administration*, 584–646.

55. Brown with Briggs and Weigle, *Hispano Folklife of New Mexico*; Marta Weigle, " 'Some New Mexico Grandmothers': A Note on the WPA Writers' Program in New Mexico," in

Weigle et al., *Hispanic Arts*, 93–102; Weigle, *New Mexicans in Cameo and Camera*, 191–93; Weigle, ed., *Two Guadalupes: Hispanic Legends and Magic Tales from Northern New Mexico* (Santa Fe: Ancient City Press, 1987); Weigle, "Finding the 'True America': Ethnic Tourism in New Mexico During the New Deal," in James Hardin and Alan Jabbour, eds., *Folklife Annual 88–89* (Washington, D.C.: American Folklife Center at the Library of Congress, 1989), 58–73; Weigle, ed., *Women of New Mexico: Depression Era Images* (Santa Fe: Ancient City Press, 1993).

56. Weigle, *New Mexicans in Cameo and Camera*, v–xviii, 214. For an overview of the FWP see McDonald, *Federal Relief Administration*, 647–750; Jerre Mangione, *The Dream and the Deal: The Federal Writers' Project, 1935–1943* (Boston: Little, Brown, 1972); Monty Noam Penkower, *The Federal Writers' Project: A Study in Government Patronage of the Arts* (Urbana: University of Illinois Press, 1977).

57. Special Coronado Cuarto Centennial edition, *Albuquerque Journal*, 30 April 1940, A–2; *Coronado Magazine: Official Program of the Coronado Cuarto Centennial in New Mexico* (Albuquerque: Valliant Printing, 1940).

58. *Coronado Cuarto Centennial: What It Will Mean to New Mexico* (Albuquerque: University of New Mexico Press, 1938), 3–4.

59. Richard L. Polese, "The Zia Sun Symbol: Variations on a Theme," *El Palacio* 75, 2 (Summer 1968): 32–33.

60. Erna Fergusson, "The Coronado Cuarto Centennial," *New Mexico Quarterly* 10 (1940): 67; *Coronado Cuarto Centennial*, 37; Edmund Sherman, "New Mexico Celebrates," *New Mexico Magazine* (June 1940): 11, 15. Also see Marta Weigle and Peter White, *The Lore of New Mexico* (Albuquerque: University of New Mexico Press, 1988), 427–33.

61. Workers of the Writers' Program of the Work Projects Administration in the State of New Mexico, comp., *New Mexico: A Guide to the Colorful State*, American Guide Series (New York: Hastings House, 1940), 166.

2. A Brief History of the Spanish Colonial Arts Society

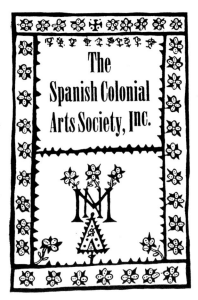

39. Cover of undated membership solicitation leaflet.

The Spanish Colonial Arts Society's certificate of incorporation was signed on October 15, 1929, the same day El Santuario at Chimayó was purchased and entrusted to the Archdiocese of Santa Fe. Official incorporation marked the end of a half decade's preservation and revival work by a small group of predominantly Anglo and mostly newcomer Santa Feans led by writer Mary Austin and artist Frank G. Applegate. The society languished following Austin's death in 1934, and it was virtually dormant until the early 1950s, when artist E. Boyd began successful revitalization efforts. Impetus for this reactivation was provided by artist and collector Cady Wells, who donated his santo collection to the Museum of New Mexico as a nucleus for a new Spanish colonial arts department. Wells stipulated that Boyd be named its curator, a position she held for the remainder of her life.[1] After E. Boyd's death in 1974 the organization continued to grow and fulfilled the basic tenets of its 1929 incorporation: the encouragement and promotion of Spanish colonial arts, their collection, exhibition and preservation, and publications and public education related to them. Mary Austin first visited Santa Fe in November 1918 "to investigate land laws and customs among Pueblo and Southwestern Indians and early Spanish and Mexican settlers."[2] Writer Ina Sizer Cassidy provided Austin with a letter of introduction to the director of the Museum of New Mexico and the School of American Research, Edgar Lee Hewett, who gave her an office in the Palace of the Governors. Austin became involved in Santa Fe's cultural activities and organized a community theater with an inaugural production on February 14, 1919. In March 1919 Austin went to Taos to visit her friend Mabel Dodge Sterne and Sterne's Taos Pueblo Indian companion Antonio Luhan. They introduced her to Penitente Brotherhood rituals at the "*morada* on Indian land not far from Mabel's house." She returned to Santa Fe after Easter and "met there a man from the Carnegie Americanization Foundation, who asked me to make a survey of the Spanish population of Taos County, which is exactly the size of the State of Maryland." Accompanied by Mabel, Tony, and artist Gustave Baumann she "went by wagon over the winter roads, and I began to get a notion of what the Spanish culture of New Mexico

40. Mary Austin and Ernest Thompson Seton at the former's house, August 7, 1927, Santa Fe, New Mexico.

41. Alice Corbin Henderson. Frame from the 1931 film, *A Day in Santa Fe,* produced by Lynn Riggs and James Hughes.

meant."[3] No such survey is extant, however, and other records indicate that through the instigation of a friend, Tucson doctor Daniel Trembly MacDougal, Austin was actually researching the northern New Mexico pueblos for Carnegie, with thought to a similar study in Arizona. She spent the summer in Taos and left New Mexico for lectures in Tucson in late November 1919 before going back to New York.[4] Mary Austin

42. John Gaw Meem presenting the deed for El Santuario de Chimayó to Archbishop Albert T. Daeger in the latter's garden, October 15, 1929. Others in attendance, from left: Paul A. F. Walter, Mrs. John Robinson of Sunmount, Dr. Francis Proctor, Alice Corbin Henderson, unidentified man, E. Dana Johnson, Mary Austin, Gustave Baumann, Marcos Chávez, Daniel T. Kelly, Judge Charles Fahy, José Chávez, Frank Applegate, Victor Ortega, Bishop Espalage, and Father Salvatore Gene of Santa Cruz.

returned to Santa Fe in the spring of 1923 and embarked on a two-thousand-mile automobile trip with Ina and Gerald Cassidy to gather notes for a book about Arizona and New Mexico similar to *The Land of Little Rain,* her 1903 essays on California. The expedition proved exhausting, and in the summer of 1923 Austin secluded herself in Taos with the now-married Luhans. In September her health was still poor when she went back to Santa Fe, where she bought property on Camino del Monte Sol before returning to New York in October 1923. *The Land of Journeys' Ending* appeared in the fall of 1924 and was well received, but Austin had neither the physical nor financial means to return to Santa Fe until March 1925, when she began to oversee construction of her house and to enjoy the company of her neighbor art colonists poet Alice Corbin Henderson; artists William Penhallow Henderson, Fremont Ellis, Joseph Bakos, and Will Shuster; and sculptor, painter, and sometime writer Frank G. Applegate and his wife Alta, who had emigrated to New Mexico from New Jersey in 1921.[5] In her obituary for Applegate, who died in 1931, Austin recalls how

we rapidly grew interested in all the old and almost dishabilitated arts of New Mexico, touched with a profound regret for their disappearance. In collecting old pieces, Frank had often recourse to native workmen for repairs, and by this means we came to realize that the capacity for handcraft, of a fine and satisfying quality, though overlaid by modern American neglect, had not completely disintegrated. We began to discuss the possibility of reviving it.

Claiming first to have used the term "Spanish Colonial" in her own writing, Austin credits *Santa Fe New Mexican* editor E. Dana Johnson with popularizing it at her insistence so that "Spanish Colonial Art became a recognized subject of interested comment in the Press." According to William Wroth, Austin thereby introduced a bias since, "in fact, all Spanish colonial crafts in New Mexico came first from Mexico, where centuries of usage distinguished many of them from the more distant Peninsular prototypes, and Southwest Indian influences must be accounted for as well." Furthermore, "the large majority of surviving examples are not colonial at all; they were made after 1821, the end of the colonial period."[6] Although seriously ill, in 1925 Austin "secured financial backing from my friend, Mrs. Elon [Blanche Ferry] Hooker [of New York City], and at a meeting at the home of Miss Manderfield (one of the Oteros) a society for the revival of Spanish Colonial Arts was launched."[7] A 1929 broadsheet identifies members of the initial group, including Austin and the Applegates, Mrs. A. S. Alvord, Sheldon Parsons, Mr. and Mrs. Datus Myers, Mr. and Mrs. Kenneth M. Chapman, Sen. Bronson M. Cutting, Mrs. Beryl Asplund, Mrs. Fenyas, Mrs. Thomas E. (Leonora S. M.) Curtin, Nina (Otero) Warren, Dr. and Mrs. Frank E. Mera, "and others." The fledgling organization, which until 1929 was often called "the Society for the Revival of the Spanish-Colonial Arts," at first "did little more than broadcast a list of examples of such crafts as might be profitable to revive and to offer prizes for new work that

conformed most exactly to the old models."

The question of what was to be revived became an issue among [society] members. A laissez-faire position, adopted by artist Andrew Dasburg and, to some extent, Frank Applegate, welcomed innovation with the attitude that the artists' work be allowed to sink or swim on its own. Others, such as industrialist Cyrus McCormick, Jr., insisted that revival work be based directly on earlier prototypes, dismissing any form of innovation. This attitude, to the extent that it was successful, restricted craftspeople to narrow antiquarian standards. . . . Some members of the society, however, cast themselves heroically as saviors of the crafts, seemingly oblivious to the fact that, for the Hispanics, the crafts did not need to be "discovered" but were well known and, in many cases, still practiced.[8]

The first exhibition sponsored by the society was held in conjunction with the annual art exhibit chaired by Mary R. Van Stone at the New (now Fine Arts) Museum during the 1926 Santa Fe Fiesta. Of the fifteen entries, those by Agua Fria artist Celso Gallegos, a carver of wood and stone, proved most popular. The 1927 Fiesta exhibition was expanded and prizes were awarded for blanket weaving, handmade furniture, figure carving, a tin *nicho,* braided rugs, hooked rugs, and crocheted pieces. Santa Fe County school superintendent Nina Otero-Warren arranged to have rural schoolchildren's work exhibited. By the 1928 Fiesta there was a Spanish colonial arts and crafts exhibition in the New Museum's reception room and a Spanish Market under the Palace of the Governors portal; Mrs. Gerald (Ina Sizer) Cassidy was in charge of the market and Mary Austin headed "Spanish Participation." Visitors from Pennsylvania and California purchased carved doors during the 1930 Fiesta.[9] Purchase of El Santuario at Chimayó was arranged in 1929 by the Society for the Revival of Spanish Arts and the Society for the Restoration and Preservation of Spanish Missions of New Mexico, groups with largely overlapping memberships, which seem to have been combined in the October incorporation of the Spanish Colonial Arts Society. Financial hardship had forced the three remaining members of the Cháves family to begin dismantling the chapel, which María de los Angeles Cháves had inherited from her mother, Carmen Abeyta, de Cháves, daughter of Bernardo Abeyta, its builder. Gustave Baumann "had discovered that the beautiful old church and its furnishings were being sold piecemeal; the small Santiago on horseback was in the hands of one curio-dealer, and the historic carved doors were being bargained for by another." *Santa Fe New Mexican* editor E. Dana Johnson was alerted, and the paper carried a spread on the situation.[10] In February or March 1929 Frank Applegate wrote about Chimayó's plight to Mary Austin in New Haven, where she was lecturing on "primitive drama" and producing a Spanish play at Yale University. According to Augusta Fink, Austin "paced the grounds of the Yale campus, praying for a solution. Then the name of a man whom she scarcely knew came to her mind. She contacted him, and within two days he had located a donor who gave the $6,000 required for purchase of the property, with

43. Lois Field, ca. 1929.

the proviso that he remain anonymous." In her obituary for Applegate, Austin recalls how "I was able to find a Catholic benefactor who made possible the purchase of the building and its content, to be held in trust by the Church for worship and as a religious museum, intact, and no alterations to be made in it without our consent." On October 15, 1929, architect John Gaw Meem delivered the Santuario deed to Archbishop Albert T. Daeger in the latter's Santa Fe garden. Present to witness the occasion were historian Paul A. F. Walter, Dr. Francis Proctor, E. Dana Johnson, Gustave Baumann, businessman Daniel T. Kelly, Judge Charles Fahy, Mrs. Frank Mera's mother Mrs. John Robinson, Alice Corbin Henderson, Frank Applegate, and Mary Austin; Chimayó residents Victor Ortega, José Cháves, and Mareos or Marcos Chávez; and Fathers Bernard Espalage, chancellor of the archdiocese, and Salvatore Gene of Santa Cruz.[11] On October 29, 1929, the certificate of incorporation for the Spanish Colonial Arts Society was filed as No. 15923 with the State Corporation Commission of New Mexico. The board of trustees included Mary Austin, Frank G. Applegate, Francis I. Proctor, George M. Bloom, Frank E. Mera, Margretta A. Dietrich, Mrs.

45. Gustave Baumann (*l.* to *r.*), John Gaw Meem, and Ernest L. Blumenschein.

A. S. Alvord, John Gaw Meem, Mary Cabot Wheelwright, Martha E. White, Mrs. Elon Hooker, Sen. Bronson M. Cutting, Mrs. Datus Myers, Mrs. Thomas E. (Leonora S. M.) Curtin, Sheldon Parsons, Benigno Muñiz, Andrew Dasburg, Archbishop Daeger, Alice Corbin Henderson, Herman Schweizer, and John D. De Huff. At the society's first meeting on November 25, 1929, Austin was elected chairman; Applegate, vice-chairman and curator; Myers, secretary; and De Huff, treasurer. Mary Austin, however, oversaw most fiscal matters until her death in 1934. Applegate also served as unpaid field-worker until

44. E. Boyd, ca. 1930.

a confidential gift in 1930 provided funds for this position. Weaver Preston E. McCrossen assumed the position of field-worker as of May 1, 1930. Together with his wife Helen Cramp McCrossen, herself a weaver, he also operated the society's newly opened shop, The Spanish Arts, in Room 39 of the Sena Plaza. This outlet was to provide a year-round market for "revival" Hispanic handwork of all kinds, and Applegate hoped it would obviate the prizes presented during the annual Santa Fe Fiestas. Throughout the shop's four-year existence, its employees administered Fiesta activities on behalf of the society. The annual Spanish Market continued as an important vehicle of Anglo patronage. According to Arrell Morgan Gibson, during this time "Mary Austin and other society members sought to promote Hispanic art by extending display and sales opportunities beyond Santa Fe and Taos...[and] were able to persuade galleries in New York, Boston, Chicago, and Kansas City to show work by Spanish-American artists from northern New Mexico."[12] The McCrossens quit The Spanish Arts in 1931 and opened their own weaving business, Kraft Shop, in a neighboring Sena Plaza room. Nellie G. Dunton took over The Spanish Arts shop, but despite her meticulous management and Mrs. Field's donation of a prize "for the best monthly contribution," the establishment could not survive slumping sales and the loss in December 1931 of McCormick's monthly donations. After February 1933 The Spanish Arts did not generate even the fifty dollars monthly rent, and it closed on October 10, 1933. Society activities came to a standstill after Mary Austin's death on August 13, 1934. Treasurer John De Huff consolidated remaining funds in August 1936. Leonora F. Curtin organized a revival on February 10, 1938, when some forty people gathered in her Acequia Madre home. Among the speakers was Harry P. Mera, who chided the society for allowing the Taylor Museum in Colorado Springs, Colorado,[13] to acquire "the best collection of Santos ever made...[because] the Society's inability to carry on was definitely the lack of funds, the problem never having been formulated, and there was never sufficient background for constructive work." Mrs. Kenneth Chapman and Reginald Fisher discussed the need for exhibition space in the Museum of New Mexico. Alice Corbin Henderson moved "that the Spanish Colonial Arts Society should be affiliated with interested Societies of the local Spanish people," an offer that Ina Sizer Cassidy seconded and that "Mrs. Ortiz accepted for the Sociedad Folklórica; Mrs. Gilbert . . . for the Lulacs." Twenty-two people joined and there was much enthusiasm though little consensus about future courses of action. **T**he energies of the revitalized society were not mobilized until the summer of 1938, when a memorandum from Edgar Lee Hewett noted that space in the Old Palace would soon become available and that "the Museum of New Mexico will welcome the help of the Spanish Colonial Arts Society in providing the public with a permanent exhibit of the finest examples obtainable of authentic New Mexico Colonial furnishings, antiques, and specimens of early weaving, handicrafts, etc." If the society proved organized enough "that there is reasonable promise of its continuance for fifty years," and if Leonora F. Curtin were to head it, "the Museum will undertake the care and fumigation of specimens and it will endeavor to provide the part time services of a curator for the listing and cataloguing of material." An accession agreement was signed on August 25, the day after two thousand pamphlets written by Paul Horgan describing the special exhibit and advertising society

46. Cady Wells, ca. 1947, Taos, New Mexico.

memberships were completed. The exhibit was Curtin's idea "because it seemed to her that as most of the old crafts pieces had been bought by dealers and private collectors, many New Mexicans had no idea what colonial New Mexican crafts were like [so] she proceeded to borrow furniture, textiles, carvings and tinwork from New Mexico friends for the show."[14] **C**are of their collection was assured by the Museum of New Mexico agreement, but the society was not as successful in placing another tangible legacy from founders Mary Austin and Frank Applegate: a jointly authored manuscript entitled "Spanish Colonial Arts." Austin's niece Mary Hunter wrote John De Huff on August 30, 1934, thanking him for the society's flowers:

The work of the Society was one of Mary Austin's deepest interests. The day before her death she told me how much she hoped the publication of the book on Spanish Colonial art by her and Frank Applegate would help your work.

Austin had "insisted on Frank's committing to paper all that he had learned about the technique of the Spanish arts," and Ansel Adams had made photographs while Applegate was still alive. Austin first approached Yale University Press in 1929, but in 1933 "hard times"

forced them to break their contract. On August 10, 1934, she sent the manuscript to Houghton Mifflin, which returned it after her death with requests for revision.[15] In 1937 and 1939 the society paid folklorist and University of New Mexico English professor T. M. Pearce to work on this ill-fated revision, which was rejected by Houghton Mifflin, by the University of New Mexico Press, and in 1939 by Walter Goodwin of Santa Fe's Rydal Press. The Laboratory of Anthropology considered the manuscript in 1941, but it was never published. **R**ecords indicate that the Spanish Colonial Arts Society was largely dormant from the late 1930s through the 1940s. Bank statements throughout the war years show an unchanging balance of $730.97; many mailings were unopened. In September 1949 Ina Sizer Cassidy wrote secretary George M. Bloom: "As there are some matters coming up for consideration of the members . . . we feel that a meeting of the Society should be called before too long." No records about these "matters" exist, and the Spanish Colonial Arts Society was not reorganized and revitalized until 1952, when E. Boyd proved as dynamic a figure as her founding predecessors, Mary Austin and Frank G. Applegate. **E**. Boyd first came to Santa Fe for three months in 1929, accompanied by her first husband Frank Andrews, whom she had met while studying and creating art in Paris.[16] After the two finalized their divorce in Philadelphia, Boyd returned alone to Santa Fe in 1930. She worked at various jobs and continued to develop her art, primarily watercolors, throughout the decade. **I**n 1936 Boyd was hired by Russell Vernon Hunter, director of the Federal Art Project of the Works Progress Administration in New Mexico, to be a watercolorist and research artist for the *Portfolio of Spanish Colonial Design in New Mexico,* which was published in an edition of two hundred copies on August 1, 1938. The experience proved pivotal for her, as she told Joy Yeck in a 1936 interview for *The WPA Reporter:*

Since living here, I have become deeply interested in the study of religious carvings and paintings in the territory, of which there is much material, and little or no information available. The more consideration the work involves the more I am convinced there should be a complete record made of this type of art. This should be done as soon as possible, as valuable pieces are constantly being sold out of the district, and others destroyed by fire, water, theft, and neglect. The materials are fragile, and have already had hard treatment. It has been a privilege to work on the present Spanish-Colonial art portfolio for the WPA, as it is directly in line with the research in which I am interested.[17]

Boyd's *Portfolio* work provided the nucleus for research that resulted in her first book, *Saints and Saintmakers of New Mexico,* designed by Merle Armitage and published in 1946 by Santa Fe's Laboratory of Anthropology. **B**y the late 1940s when she moved to Los Angeles, E. Boyd had become a recognized authority on New Mexican Spanish colonial art. First an assistant to the owner of the Hispano-American Bookstore, she then worked as research librarian and later as registrar for the Los Angeles County Museum. When her friend Cady Wells decided to

47. Alan C. Vedder, ca. 1976.
48. Ann H. Vedder, ca. 1980.

donate his extensive santo collection, which Boyd had advised him on and had catalogued, to the Museum of New Mexico, he stipulated that the museum set up a separate department for Spanish colonial art and hire a curator who met his approval. Wells's recommendation of E. Boyd was accepted by museum director Boaz Long, and she began to work for the museum in 1952. Rallying others to the protection and preservation of Spanish colonial art was one of her first concerns. According to Claudia Larcombe:

Aware that the by then inactive Spanish Colonial Arts Society. . .was incorporated only until 1979, she took it upon herself to "reanimate the society in 1952." This was not an easy task; first it involved finding members of the original group and convincing them that the newly interested people "were not a rival society nor [did they have] dishonest intentions." Then old board members had to be asked to resign, notices had to be published in the newspaper, and new volunteers found to supplement the membership. The reactivated society was then able to collect money as a nonprofit organization and to spend it on Spanish colonial art and restoration. The importance of this becomes more evident when one realizes that, in the early years, the museum's Spanish colonial art department was appropriated only two hundred dollars a year for new acquisitions and that, since the society's holdings were housed at the museum, the department was able to use a much larger collection for research and exhibition. In part through the help of the Spanish Colonial Arts Society, E. Boyd was able to build a substantial collection of santos for the museum.[18]

The first official revitalization and reorganization meeting was held on February 14, 1952. Lois Field became interim president, briefly succeeded by E. Boyd; permanent officers, led by president Wayne L. Mauzy and a sixteen-member board of trustees, were elected at a general membership meeting on June 16, 1952. The reorganized society continued the collection, preservation, exhibition, and publication work of the earlier group. E. Boyd's curatorial work was conducted first at the Fine Arts Museum and later at the Museum of International Folk Art, which opened in 1953. In the early 1950s Boyd was joined by Alan C. Vedder, a Bostonian who came to Santa Fe following a bout with tuberculosis. He asked E. Boyd to evaluate a retablo he wanted to purchase. She "immediately recognized his discerning eye for detail and convinced him to volunteer one day a week, [and] his talents as a conservator and tolerance for tedious work secured his place as Boyd's assistant." Vedder became a conservator for the Museum of New Mexico and in 1965 replaced Boyd as curator of the Spanish Colonial Arts Society. Together with his wife, native Santa Fean Ann Healy, whom he married in 1962, he assembled a large personal collection of Spanish colonial, Latin American, and Spanish art and "encouraged others to make bequests of private collections, either to the Museum or the Society." The two actively and tirelessly "encouraged Hispanic artists to rediscover and revive Spanish Colonial traditional arts."[19]
In 1954 the society contributed funds for restoring the Oratorio de San Buenaventura on the old Plaza del Cerro at Chimayó. This private

chapel belonged to the Ortega family and was left to the Archdiocese of Santa Fe by Bonifacia Ortega. With materials purchased with society funds and labor supplied by members of the Confraternity of Our Lady of Carmel under the direction of Merejildo Jaramillo, the project was completed in November 1954.[20] Other society funds allocated for architectural conservation projects were used to rebuild an Ojo Caliente church in 1956 and to restore St. Francis Cathedral's La Conquistadora Chapel in 1956 and 1957. In 1961 the society received from Ruth Catlin a gift of 3.2 acres of land adjacent to St. John's College in Santa Fe, but the society was never able to establish a contextual museum to showcase its expanding collection. A February 12, 1962, letter from the Museum of New Mexico discouraged the society's efforts, according to Ann Vedder, because they were ''in conflict with the state museum's plans for the Palace of the Governors . . . to include room- and building-replica displays of a chapel, gristmill, homes, and shops, as well as other replica units around and in the expanded palace patio.'' Only the chapel and one period room were completed by E. Boyd in the Palace of the Governors, although ''the letter indicated that such displays would be installed as soon as possible and would bring out of storage the bulk of the collections in the museum's custody, including materials then covered by long-term loan agreements such as that in effect between the museum and the Spanish Colonial Arts Society.''[21] An agreement between the society and the School of American Research for loan of the collection had been executed on April 21, 1954, but was terminated by mutual consent. The society and the Museum of New Mexico signed a new loan agreement on May 4, 1961, ''for a period ending October 30, 1979, a date coinciding with the end of the then corporate existence of the society, which had been incorporated in 1929 with a term of fifty years.'' An amended certificate of incorporation allowing for ''perpetual existence'' and bylaws were finally completed, approved, and filed in 1977, by which time the committee negotiating a long-term loan with the Museum of New Mexico began work in earnest. A twenty-year loan agreement was signed on November 1, 1979. At this time too, Lois Field's son William assumed the presidency of the society.[22] By the late 1960s plans were well under way for a living museum at the La Cienega ranch of society members Y. A. Paloheimo, a Finnish diplomat, and his wife Leonora F. Curtin. Beginning in 1954 the Spanish Colonial Arts Society served as repository for objects purchased by the Paloheimos and other board members specifically for future use in this museum. When El Rancho de las Golondrinas opened in the spring of 1972, it included objects on loan from the society's collection.[23] The society has continued to contribute to Las Golondrinas, most recently with a donation in 1991 toward purchase of a seventeenth-century Spanish colonial home site in La Cienega.[24] The annual Fiesta Spanish markets of the 1920s and early 1930s were revived in 1965, when during Indian Market the society sponsored a Native Spanish Market under the portal of the First National Bank on the Santa Fe plaza. There was no Spanish Market in 1966, but from 1967 until 1971 Spanish Market and Indian Market took place on the same August weekend. Indian Market grew, and thus both events could not occur at the same time. Spanish Market was subsequently moved to the last weekend in July and was held under the portal at the Palace of the Governors. A children's category was inaugurated in 1981. Because the simultaneous, annual Contemporary Hispanic Market was begun in the patio of the Palace of the Governors in 1985 and moved adjacent to the society's Spanish Market on Lincoln Avenue in 1990, the latter has become known as Traditional Spanish Market. Winter Spanish Market was organized initially in conjunction with the short-lived Winter Indian Market in 1989 and has since been held during the first weekend in December at Santa Fe's La Fonda Hotel. For the most part, Spanish Market as characterized by Ann Vedder still prevails:

Since the revival of the market, members of the society, especially its curators . . . , have worked diligently with exhibitors and other crafts[people] to develop their interests and skills in traditional Spanish colonial crafts. The result has been an improvement in those crafts and an expansion in their types. . . . In keeping with the society's stated purposes, all the crafts must be traditional. Innovations are not discouraged, but, since there are many other avenues and outlets for nontraditional and contemporary crafts, the society has felt it proper to adhere quite strictly to its stated purposes.[25]

Spanish Colonial Arts Society publications have appeared sporadically: in May 1954 E. Boyd's twenty-page pamphlet, *Hand List of the Collection of the Spanish Colonial Arts Society;* in 1956 the thirty-two-page pamphlet containing *El Palacio* articles by Stephen F. de Borhegyi and E. Boyd, *El Santuario de Chimayo;* in 1966 a reprint of Kate Chapman and Dorothy N. Stewart's forty-page, 1930 pamphlet, *Adobe Notes, or How to Keep the Weather Out with Just Plain Mud,* originally printed on Spud Johnson's Laughing Horse Press in Taos; and in 1972 the sixteen-page, bilingual *El leon y el grillito: The Lion and The Cricket,* a facsimile of a nineteenth-century Spanish fable told by C. S. Suarez. The most ambitious project until this volume has been *Hispanic Arts and Ethnohistory in the Southwest: New Papers Inspired by the Work of E. Boyd,* edited by Marta Weigle with Claudia Larcombe and Samuel Larcombe and jointly published in clothbound and paperback editions by Ancient City Press, Santa Fe, and the University of New Mexico Press, Albuquerque, in 1983. This 423-page collection of twenty-two new papers on E. Boyd, on Hispanic arts, on preservation, and on Hispano ethnohistory was selected for inclusion in the 1984 Western Books Exhibition of fine printing sponsored by the Rounce and Coffin Club of Los Angeles. E. Boyd's authoritative study of Hispanic religious and domestic arts and crafts was published by the Museum of New Mexico Press, Santa Fe, in 1974. She called it *Popular Arts of Spanish New Mexico* because, as she told Samuel Larcombe: ''Folk, folk, folk: nasty old German word— I hate it. 'Popular' is from the Latin, all the way back to classical days, and Latin is the source of Spanish and popular is like populace; the

49. Ann Vedder (*l.* to *r.*), David Ortega, E. Boyd, unidentified woman, and Alan C. Vedder outside the Ortega family's San Buenaventura Chapel, Chimayó Plaza, Chimayó, New Mexico, 1970.

people."[26] Boyd's death on September 30, 1974, deeply affected but did not cripple the society. Boyd's work for the society was ably continued and advanced by Alan and Ann Vedder. Alan Vedder published *Furniture of Spanish New Mexico* with Santa Fe's Sunstone Press in 1977 and served as society curator from 1965 until 1989. Ann Healy Vedder died on January 24, 1989, Alan C. Vedder on December 8 of that year. Spanish Colonial Arts Society president William Field wrote on December 15:

As I looked around the church at yesterday's memorial service for Alan Vedder, I saw so many who had been influenced, perhaps "strong-armed," by Alan and Ann to become involved in the preservation of the arts, crafts, traditions and architecture of our state. The effect the two of them have had on so many of us is immeasurable.

The leadership, thoughtfulness, guidance and conscience that Alan and Ann brought to the activities of the Spanish Colonial Arts Society is legend. Since E. Boyd died, they have been the Society, with the rest of us following their lead so gratefully and with such appreciation for their deep interest in everything the Society was involved in.

In late 1988 Donna Pierce, then board member and society secretary, had begun a piece-by-piece inventory of and interviews with both Vedders about the society collections. Ann Vedder died two months after the interviews began and most of the ten, ninety-minute tapes completed in October 1989 were with Alan, who died before the inventory was finished.[27] The Ann and Alan Vedder Estate enabled the Spanish Colonial Arts Society to continue all aspects of its work, to initiate this publication, and to move its office on June 1, 1992, to 239½ Johnson Street in downtown Santa Fe. It houses the Vedder Lending Library, whose books may be checked out for one month by members and Spanish Market artists, and has "become an active sales office for Spanish Market posters, magazines, notecards, SCAS memberships, and donated art items from the Spanish Market artists." Since 1988 Bud Redding has served as executive director of the society, assisted since November 1991 by Patricia A. Price. Donna Pierce became curator in January 1990. From 1983 until early 1993, carver and antiques restorer Ray Herrera served on the board of directors and as market manager.[28] On April 2, 1993, a few of the hundreds in attendance at the blessing of the restored *Morada del Alto* at Abiquiú were reminded of the October 15, 1929, ceremony involving the newly formed society and the deed for El Santuario de Chimayó. The Abiquiú Penitente *morada*, dating from the nineteenth century and one of the oldest in the state, had been heinously robbed, torched, and defiled with Satanic symbols in September 1992.[29] According to Carmella M. Padilla:

The crime, which remains unsolved, drew the attention of the entire state, and scores of volunteers mobilized to help mend the desecrated building and the devastated community. The Spanish Colonial Arts Society immediately threw its support behind the project, joining with the New Mexico Community Foundation and Recursos de Santa Fe in establishing the Abiquiú Morada Restoration Fund. Now, ten months and $23,000 later, the morada *stands resurrected where it once stood in ruin.*

"This is the start of a new chapter in the life of this building and all that it symbolizes," said Charlie Carrillo, a Santa Fe santero *[saint-maker] who has been a member of Abiquiú's penitente brotherhood since 1979. "But more important, this has been an education into an important part of our history and our Hispanic heritage."[30]*

The Spanish Colonial Arts Society is governed by a board of directors that in 1994 included Nancy Meem Wirth and William Field, both long associated with the organization. For the first time, Hispanics are serving in the highest board positions: Fred Cisneros as president and Carmella Padilla and F. Christopher Olivera as vice-presidents. Artist and photographer Cisneros stated "that the society didn't have a Hispanic president in its previous 67 years is not a sign of racism . . . [but] a lack of real education among the Hispanic community and a misperception of what it is."[31] Among the first Hispanic members of the reorganized Spanish Colonial Arts Society and now an honorary board member was native Santa Fean and longtime schoolteacher Anita Gonzales Thomas, honored at the 41st Annual Traditional Spanish Market on July 25–26, 1992. As Anita Gonzales, Thomas learned *colcha* embroidery from an elderly aunt and won a blue ribbon for a *colcha* bedspread exhibited in the 1933 Spanish Market. She joined the society in the late 1960s "to support a group that was interested in seeing that this tradition, this art, wouldn't disappear." In 1982, at Ann and Alan Vedder's urging, she became a board member, recalling: "I felt it was very important to contribute a Hispanic element to the board because I felt I could be a bridge between the Hispanic artists and the Society—which was mostly Anglo—since I was able to work comfortably with both." Her concerns for the future, "the importance of involving a new generation of Hispanics in both the Spanish Market and the Society," are shared by many: "We must emphasize to our youth—both artists and non-artists—that this organization is really doing something worthwhile. We have to let them know their heritage is something to be proud of, and that they're responsible for making sure it survives after people like me leave this world behind."[32]

NOTES

1. Most material for this brief history comes from Marta Weigle, ''The First Twenty-Five Years of the Spanish Colonial Arts Society,'' and Ann Vedder, ''History of the Spanish Colonial Arts Society, Inc., 1951–1981,'' in Weigle with Claudia Larcombe and Samuel Larcombe, eds., *Hispanic Arts and Ethnohistory in the Southwest: New Papers Inspired by the Work of E. Boyd* (Santa Fe: Ancient City Press; Albuquerque: University of New Mexico Press, 1983), 181–217. Archival records and ephemera documented in those articles are not referenced below; only published and new sources are cited. Records for the first twenty-five years are in the Papers of the Spanish Colonial Arts Society, New Mexico State Records Center and Archives, Santa Fe; others are in the files at the society's Santa Fe office.

2. *El Palacio* 5, 15 (2 November 1918): 254, as cited in Marta Weigle and Kyle Fiore, *Santa Fe and Taos: The Writer's Era, 1916–1941* (Santa Fe: Ancient City Press, 1982), 13.

3. Mary Austin, *Earth Horizon: Autobiography* (Boston: Houghton Mifflin, 1932), 340.

4. Augusta Fink, *I-Mary: A Biography of Mary Austin* (Tucson: University of Arizona Press, 1983), 185–86, 187, 190–92. Suzanne Forrest notes that ''the Carnegie Foundation has no record of Austin's study having ever been done, Sarah Deutsch, personal correspondence, 20 August 1985'' (*The Preservation of the Village: New Mexico's Hispanics and the New Deal* [Albuquerque: University of New Mexico Press, 1989], 195n20).

5. Fink, *I-Mary,* 209–16, 219, 223–25, 226.

6. Mary Austin, ''Frank Applegate,'' *New Mexico Quarterly* 2 (1932): 214; William Wroth, ''The Hispanic Craft Revival in New Mexico,'' in Janet Kardon, ed., *Revivals! Diverse Traditions, 1920–1945: The History of Twentieth-Century American Craft* (New York: Harry N. Abrams with the American Craft Museum, 1994), 85–86.

7. Austin, ''Applegate,'' 214.

8. Wroth, ''Hispanic Craft Revival,'' 86

9. ''The Santa Fe Fiesta—1926,'' *El Palacio* 21 (1926): 97; ''Museum Events: Spanish Colonial Arts,'' *El Palacio* 23 (1927): 337–39; ''Santa Fe Fiesta: Events at Gallup and Albuquerque,'' *El Palacio* 25 (1928): 183; *Santa Fe New Mexican,* 27 August 1930, as cited in Arrell Morgan Gibson, *The Santa Fe and Taos Colonies: Age of the Muses, 1900–1942* (Norman: University of Oklahoma Press, 1983), 173.

10. Alice Corbin Henderson, ''E. Dana Johnson: June 15, 1879–December 10, 1937,'' *New Mexico Historical Review* 13 (1938): 123.

11. Fink, *I-Mary,* 239–40; Austin, ''Applegate,'' 215. The photo appears in Daniel T. Kelly with Beatrice Chauvenet, *The Buffalo Head: A Century of Mercantile Pioneering in the Southwest* (Santa Fe: Vergara Publishing, 1972), opposite p. 192. Beatrice Chauvenet describes the transaction and the occasion in *John Gaw Meem: Pioneer in Historic Preservation* (Santa Fe: Historic Santa Fe Foundation/Museum of New Mexico Press, 1985), 67–68.

12. Gibson, *Santa Fe and Taos Colonies,* 173.

13. Mera presumably refers to Harry Garnett's collection, begun in May 1936, of Arroyo Hondo folk art from the village's five religious structures: Our Lady of Sorrows Church, the two Penitente Brotherhood *moradas,* and the two private chapels of the prominent Martínez and Medina families (Robert L. Shalkop, *Arroyo Hondo: The Folk Art of a New Mexican Village* [Colorado Springs: Taylor Museum of the Colorado Springs Fine Arts Center, 1969]).

14. Sarah Nestor, *The Native Market of the Spanish New Mexican Craftsmen, Santa Fe, 1933–1940* (Santa Fe: Colonial New Mexico Historical Foundation, 1978), 51. Curtin ''was asked to reproduce the exhibit for the New Mexico entry at the New York World''s Fair of 1939–40, . . . [but] declined out of respect for the safety of treasures in the possession of people who loved them—and the state went unrepresented.'' (ibid.).

15. Fink, *I-Mary,* 240, 253, 255, 257. Also see T. M. Pearce, *Literary America, 1903–1934: The Mary Austin Letters* (Westport, Conn.: Greenwood Press, 1979), 217–18.

16. This material comes from Claudia Larcombe, ''E. Boyd: A Biographical Sketch,'' in Weigle et al., *Hispanic Arts and Ethnohistory,* 3–13.

17. Joy Yeck, ''New Mexico WPA Art Program Includes E. Boyd Hall Doing Important Work,'' *The WPA Reporter,* Works Progress Administration for New Mexico (April 1936): 8 (copy in E. Boyd Collection, New Mexico State Records Center and Archives, Santa Fe).

18. Larcombe, ''E. Boyd,'' 9. Larcombe quotes from a 14 July 1954 letter from E. Boyd to Dr. and Mrs. Pál Kelemen.

19. ''Vedders Leave Legacy of Excellence,'' *Spanish Market,* (Santa Fe: Spanish Colonial Arts Society for the 1990 Spanish Market): 8.

20. E. Boyd, ''Repair of the Oratorio of San Buenaventura at Chimayó, Co-Sponsored by the Spanish Colonial Arts Society,'' *El Palacio* 62, 4 (April 1955): 99–101. Additional maintenance and preservation funds were donated in 1963 and 1969. Thieves stole the chapel's bell in the mid-1970s, and society members joined villagers and Smithsonian Institution representatives to secure another, which was blessed and first rung in October 1993 (Don Unser, ''A New Bell Chimes in Chimayó,'' *Spanish Market: The Magazine of the Spanish Colonial Arts Society, Inc.* (July 1994): 43.

21. Vedder, ''History,'' 209–10.

22. Ibid., 207, 212–13. The following have served as president of the reorganized society: Lois Field (interim, February–March 1952), E. Boyd (interim, March–June 1952), Wayne L. Mauzy (June 1952–May 1957), Erik K. Reed (May 1957–May 1962), no president for various administrative reasons (May 1962–May 1964), Sallie Wagner (May 1964–May 1967), George Roy (May 1967–May 1971), Samuel Larcombe (May 1971–May 1972), Mrs. Walter L. Goodwin, Jr. (May 1972–May 1977), Don J. Madtson (May 1977–November 1979), William Field (November 1979–May 1991), Paul D. Gerber (May 1991–May 1993), Fred Cisneros (May 1993–May 1995), Carmella Padilla (May 1995–).

23. Harriet Kimbro, ''Las Golondrinas,'' *New Mexico Magazine,* (July/August 1974): 14–19; Louann Jordan and St. George Cooke, *El Rancho de las Golondrinas: Spanish Colonial Life in New Mexico* (Santa Fe: Colonial New Mexico Historical Foundation, 1977). Thomas Curtin purchased four hundred acres from the Baca family in 1932. It was leased to the Colonial New Mexico Historical Foundation in 1971.

24. Known as LA 20,000, this site is being excavated by Colorado College students under the direction of Marianne L. Stoller and David H. Snow. Efforts by Stoller, Snow, and the late Myra Ellen Jenkins have resulted in its purchase and deeding to El Rancho de las Golondrinas for future development as a museum.

25. Vedder, ''History,'' 211.

26. Larcombe, ''E. Boyd,'' 11.

27. William Field letter of 15 December 1989 reproduced in ''Vedders Leave Legacy''; Carmella M. Padilla, ''Eye on the SCAS Collection: Donna Pierce carries on Boyd, Vedder legacies,'' *Spanish Market,* (Santa Fe: Spanish Colonial Arts Society for the 1993 Spanish Market): 5–6.

28. *Spanish Colonial Arts Society Noticias,* newsletter, 1992; Kay Bird, ''Spanish Market Honors Herrera for What Comes Naturally: Life Preserved,'' *Santa Fe New Mexican,* 25 July 1993, E–1.

29. Bainbridge Bunting, Thomas R. Lyons, Margil Lyons, ''Penitente Brotherhood Moradas and Their Architecture,'' in Weigle et al., *Hispanic Arts and Ethnohistory,* 58. Also see Richard Eighme Ahlborn, *The Penitente Moradas of Abiquiú* (1968; reprint, Washington, D.C.: Smithsonian Institution Press, 1986).

30. Carmella M. Padilla, ''SCAS Helps Bring Morada Back from the Ashes,'' *Spanish Market,* 1993, 33.

31. Kay Bird, ''Something New at Traditional Spanish Market: Hispanics Take Over Leadership of Board,'' *Santa Fe New Mexican,* 24 July 1993, B–1. The 1994–95 board included president Fred Cisneros, vice presidents Carmella Padilla and F. Christopher Olivera, secretary Nancy Meem Wirth, treasurer William Ashbey, and members Ed Berry, Richard Casillas, Anneke Chittim, Dr. Julio Dávila, William Field, Paul Gerber, Gayle Kartozian, Susan Harrison Kelly, Mac Lewis, Rey Móntez, Sandy Osterman, Jack Parsons, Charles Pineda, Barbara Torres, and Robert Worcester. Honorary board members are Susan Girard, Virginia Goodwin, Marjorie Lambert, Don J. Madtson, Anita Gonzales Thomas, and Marta Weigle.

32. All quotations and material from Carmella M. Padilla, ''Anita Thomas: Spanish Market's Grande Dame,'' *Spanish Market,* (Santa Fe: Spanish Colonial Arts Society for the 1992 Spanish Market): 8–9.

3. Revival Period Arts and Artists

CARMELLA PADILLA

The Spanish Colonial Arts Society was launched in late 1925. Its initial efforts to "broadcast a list of examples of such crafts as might be profitable to revive and to offer prizes for new work that conformed most exactly to the old models" materialized the following summer. Spanish Market, at first called Spanish Fair or Spanish Colonial Arts and Crafts Exhibition, began in conjunction with the 1926 Santa Fe Fiesta at the Museum of New Mexico's Fine Arts Museum.[1] The works exhibited were not considered new, but the attempt to bring their creators into public view was unprecedented. Only fifteen entries, mostly carvings of religious images in wood and stone, were displayed. Nevertheless, the small, simple exhibit marked the beginning of several decades of effort by the Spanish Colonial Arts Society to provide artistic and economic outlets for regional Hispanics working in the traditional arts. Some of the artists whom the society encouraged early on were those who had continued to produce traditional wares even during the traditions' decline in the late nineteenth century. Notable among these artists was santero Celso Gallegos (1864–1943).[2]

CELSO GALLEGOS

Born in the tiny village of Agua Fria west of Santa Fe, Gallegos was a devout man who lived next door to the village church of San Isidro and served for many years as church sacristan and *resador velorios,* or reader of prayers. Family legend maintains that his great-great-grandfather had worked as a santero in the late eighteenth century. As a young man Gallegos inherited a bulto thought to have been made by his great-great-grandfather. According to family oral tradition the inherited bulto, a rococo-style polychrome, was thought to be of Saint Bartholomew. Although the bulto was probably based on Mexican crèche genre figures, it greatly influenced the carvings Gallegos created. Working mostly in pine, often partly rotted or with a large knot, he often produced images that are distinguished by a twist or hunch similar to that in the inherited bulto. In the early twentieth century he carved his own bulto of Saint Bartholomew, a figure that perfectly illustrates similarities to his great-great-grandfather's work. Gallegos thus adopted from the late eighteenth-century rococo a long-outdated artistic convention, an exaggerated body twist, and made it an element of twentieth-century Hispanic wood carving. Although he used traditional imagery and iconography,

50

51

50. Celso Gallegos, *Our Lady of Mt. Carmel* (r.) and *Christ Child* (l., top and bottom), ca. 1930–39, Agua Fria, New Mexico. Stone. Purchased in memory of E. Boyd. **51.** Celso Gallegos, *St. George and the Dragon*, ca. 1930–39, Agua Fria, New Mexico. Pine, varnish. Formerly in collection of Eleanor Bedell; bequest of Alan and Ann Vedder. **52.** Attributed to Celso Gallegos's great-great-grandfather, *Unidentified male figure*, ca. 1790–1820, Mexico or New Mexico. Wood, gesso, paint. Purchased from Gallegos' granddaughter, Dora Tapia. Although this image may be a genre figure from a crèche made in Mexico, family oral history attributes it to Gallegos's great-great-grandfather and called it St. Bartholomew. **53.** Celso Gallegos, *Christ Child of Atocha,* ca. 1930–39, Agua Fria, New Mexico. Piñon wood, wood stain, varnish. Purchased from Dora Tapia. **54.** Celso Gallegos, *Virgin and Child,* ca. 1930–39, Agua Fria, New Mexico. Cottonwood, oil paint. Slight body twist is distinctive of Gallegos. **55.** Celso Gallegos, *Unidentified male figure,* ca. 1930–39, Agua Fria, New Mexico. Pine, varnish, paint. Gift of Mr. and Mrs. John Gaw Meem. With distinctive body twist and hunched back, this figure was based on the image (52.) once owned by Gallegos's family. **56.** Celso Gallegos, *Nativity,* 1925, Agua Fria, New Mexico. Pine, varnish. Dated. Gift of Morris Burge.

52   53   54   55

56

Gallegos introduced numerous innovations to the New Mexican woodcarving tradition. His trademark twist was unusual among other New Mexican santero work, which was more commonly symmetrical and flat. Whether by personal choice or through encouragement from Anglo patrons, he used only small amounts of paint, without a gesso ground, on his images. Gallegos was fond of noting that the only tool he used to carve was a simple pocketknife. Carving in wood and occasionally stone, he was prolific, and his varied works include figures in the round and on flat panels. His extensive execution of cutout panels was another stylistic innovation, in some ways a merging of the bulto and retablo traditions. Besides religious images, Gallegos carved animals, cemetery markers, walking canes, and wooden finger rings. He also painted on canvas and did *colcha* embroidery. The inaugural 1926 Spanish Market was Gallegos's first public exhibition, and his works proved most popular. He took first prize in the carving category at the 1926 and 1927 markets, as well as in later years. In a 1931 article in *El Pasatiempo* he was cited as "one of the best known and beloved of the native craftsmen, and one of the most skilled." When Gallegos died on April 6, 1943, he had been acclaimed in various exhibitions and publications. Although hundreds of his works are lost, a number are included in the Spanish Colonial Arts Society collection and attest to

58

59

57

the depth and skill of a man whose faith and extraordinary works inspired generations to come. One who was particularly touched by Gallegos's skill and devotion was José Dolores López, a Córdova carpenter who himself became one of the greatest New Mexico wood-carvers.[3] Like Gallegos, López was a pious man who served as church sacristan. His talents brought him to the attention of Mary Austin, Frank Applegate, and other Santa Fe patrons, most of them associated with the Spanish Colonial Arts Society. Born in 1868 into a family of wood-carvers in Córdova, the same mountain village where the acclaimed nineteenth-century santero José Rafael Aragón had practiced his craft, López was a farmer and wood-carver himself. According to family oral tradition he became more serious about wood carving in 1917 to divert his attention from worries about his son Nicudemos's service in World War I. López's initial woodworking efforts, starting with pine furniture finished in brightly colored house paints, were created to meet the needs of local villagers. Chairs, chests, *trasteros* (cabinets), and *relojeros* (clock shelves) were standards in his repertoire. After López's so-called discovery by Santa Fe patrons in the early 1920s, his style changed dramatically. Frank

JOSÉ DOLORES LÓPEZ
ca. 1935

57. José Dolores López, *Flight into Egypt,* ca. 1926–38, Córdova, New Mexico. Cottonwood, pine, cotton fabric, leather. Gift of Mary Cabot Wheelwright. **58.** José Dolores López, Chest, ca. 1920–38, Córdova, New Mexico. Pine, black oil paint stain. Gift of Mrs. Laura Hersloff. **59.** José Dolores López, Table, ca. 1920–38, Córdova, New Mexico. Pine. Signed, made by López for Dorothy Stuart. Acquired from estate of Margretta Dietrich; bequest of Alan and Ann Vedder. **60.** José Dolores López, Straw appliqué cross, ca. 1920–38, Córdova, New Mexico. Cedar, straw, green stain, commercial glue. Signed in pencil: "José D. López Córdoba N.M."; reverse covered with incised designs. **61.** José Dolores López, Screen door, late 1920s, Córdova, New Mexico. Pine, cedar, paint. Gift of Mr. and Mrs. William Field. **62.** José Dolores López, *Animal Orchestra,* ca. 1920–38, Córdova, New Mexico. Pine. Gift of Mary Cabot Wheelwright. Signed in pencil: "J. D. López, Córdova." **63.** José Dolores López, Lazy Susan, 1929–33, Córdova, New Mexico. Pine. Acquired at Spanish Market between 1929–33; gift of Lois Field. Signed in pencil: "José D. López/ Las Córdovas".

61

60

62

63

39

Applegate persuaded him to sell his works at the Santa Fe Fiesta. However, when López's crude polychrome technique proved too gaudy for the Santa Fe buyers, he was encouraged to leave his work unpainted. Family legend claims this was when López integrated his skill as a filigree jeweler into his woodwork. Using chip carving and incised filigree-like designs to emphasize the detail, López developed and refined an original style, one considered quite contemporary for the era. He concentrated on furniture and incorporated the ornate new style into his standard pieces, such as chests and bookshelves, as well as into newer, non-traditional objects as lazy Susans, record racks, and even screen doors. The bird-and-leaf motifs López often etched into his furniture inspired his next woodworking venture: carved animals. In an effort to make them as lifelike as possible, López often heavily embellished birds, squirrels, mice, cats, and pigs with chip carving to accentuate facial and bodily features. Other animal carvings were influenced by Swiss and German toys that Nicudemos had brought back after the war. In the whimsical *Animal Orchestra* five animals sit on the edge of a table playing instruments while a squirrel heads for a bird sitting atop a central pole. In most cases, however, López placed his animal figurines upon tree branches bursting with finely detailed leaves. Trees and leaves became other characteristic elements in his ever-expanding vocabulary of motifs. López's imagery is thought to have been secular until 1929, when Frank Applegate, mindful of the carver's deep Catholic faith, encouraged him to try his hand at religious bultos. López was inspired by his faith and by José Rafael Aragón's images that adorned the Córdova church. Unlike Aragón, who used paint to stress particular features and expressions, López employed precise, chip-carved filigree designs to bring his figures to life. This approach demonstrates his stylistic departure from traditions of the eighteenth- and nineteenth-century santeros. López carved religious images only during the last decade of his life. Because these works were his most complex and ambitious—some were made from hundreds of separate hand-carved pieces—they are the images for which he is best known. *Nacimientos* (nativity scenes), the *Flight into Egypt,* and depictions of Saint Peter, Adam and Eve, Saint Michael the Archangel, Saint Anthony, and Our Lady of Light were common themes in his oeuvre. He also produced a number of death carts, which are believed to have been influenced by one made by his father, Nasario López, a nineteenth-century Cordova carver.[4] A signed straw appliqué cross is yet another example of the artist's versatility. López's elegant, unpainted style and his eagerness to experiment reveal his individualistic orientation. He relied on facial expressions, body gestures, and crisp, chip-carved detail to evoke the drama of his religious subjects. His inventive use of contrasting native woods, such as aspen, cedar, and pine enhanced his subjects. By the time of his death in 1937 López's work had appeared in numerous publications and exhibitions and he was revered throughout the region as the innovator of a thoroughly modern carving style known as the Córdova style. While the Córdova

style was considered contemporary for the era, it was quickly established as traditional in the tiny village itself. López died not long after refining his technique, but had taught his skills to his children Liria, George, Ricardo, and Nicudemos, all of whom were eager to continue working in his distinctive style. Fully aware of the vital commercial enterprise he had created for his family, López generated a lineage of highly skilled wood-carvers who continue to benefit from his efforts. Although all the López children excelled in their carving, only George López, who was born in 1900 and began carving in 1925, would become as well known as his father. Working alongside his father with many of his works as prototypes, George López's early carvings were strikingly similar. A comparison of George's *Flight into Egypt* with a carving of the same subject by José Dolores clearly illustrates the resemblance. Nonetheless, George's *Flight into Egypt* reveals the emergence of a personal style. Although perhaps not as refined as his father's at this early stage, George's work was much more elaborate, as seen in the staff, the carpenter's tool box, and the base. The younger López's figures are also more blocklike and massive. From the time of José Dolores's death in 1937 until 1952, George López's carving took a backseat to his job at Los Alamos National Laboratory (LANL). He simplified his work by reducing the amount of filigree ornamentation on each piece. After his retirement from LANL, however, he worked full-time refining his technique to equal the precision and complexity his father had achieved. George's repertoire at this stage included many religious images as well as the complex *Tree of Life,* one of which he created from 395 separate pieces. With his wife Silvianita Trujillo, George López also refined his entrepreneurial skills and set up a shop in his house. With time to produce a large inventory of work, he became the first Córdova santero to make carving his primary source of income. By 1960 George López was internationally known as Córdova's leading santero. He died in the village in 1993 at the age of ninety-three. Although not as renowned, other members of the López family continued to carve in the Córdova style after George's death. Ricardo and Rafael López were just as prolific as their brother George and they also set up shop in Córdova. However, since both brothers worked at Los Alamos National Laboratory until retirement, they sold their work under their wives' names. Ricardo's was signed in his wife Benita López's name, while Rafael sold under that of his wife Precidez López. Stylistically it is clear that their works were made in the original López family tradition. For example, a cedar *Santo Niño with Birds,* signed by Benita López, employs the familiar López family leaves and birds. Rafael and Precidez López also carved trees and animals until their deaths in 1968. More recently, Ricardo López has been recognized for his own works and for developing new styles in the Córdova genre. He is noted as one of the few family wood-carvers to make flowers. His red-and-white–cedar *Flower,* which is in the Spanish Colonial Arts Society collection, exemplifies his artistry and skill. During the late 1920s and early 1930s, while Hispanic artists Celso

64. George López, *Flight into Egypt,* before 1941, Córdova, New Mexico. Pine, white cedar, leather. Gift of Amelia E. White. Signed in pencil: *"[H]echo por George López precio $14.50 [h]echo por Córdova N. Mex.,"* "Made by George López price $14.50 made in Córdova, N. Mex." **65.** Ricardo López, *Flower,* 1979, Córdova, New Mexico. Cedar. Gift of artist. **66.** Lorenzo López, *Cart with Oxen,* ca. 1930–49, Santa Fe, New Mexico. Pine, willow, leather. Purchased from artist's son, Juan Pablo López. **67.** Alfonso Griego, *Fred Astaire,* 1965, Santa Fe, New Mexico. Wood. Bequest of Alan and Ann Vedder. **68.** Apolonio O. Martínez, *St. James (Santiago),* 1975, Chimayó, New Mexico. Aspen, pine, leather. Purchased at Spanish Market 1975. **69.** Benita López, *Tree of Life with Christ Child,* 1972, Córdova, New Mexico. White cedar. Awarded honorable mention and purchased at Spanish Market 1972. **70.** Sigfried Martínez, *St. James (Santiago),* 1960, Chimayó, New Mexico. Wood, leather. Bequest of Alan and Ann Vedder. **71.** Leandro Montoya, *St. Isidore (San Isidro),* 1960, Santa Fe, New Mexico. Wood. Signed. Bequest of Alan and Ann Vedder.

GEORGE LÓPEZ
January, 1958

Gallegos and the Córdova carvers infused new life into longstanding traditions, the Spanish Colonial Arts Society continued to seek ways to provide them with new opportunities.[5] In a short-lived effort to create a year-round market for the traditional arts, the society opened The Spanish Arts shop in Santa Fe's Sena Plaza in 1930. It closed in October 1933, but in June 1934 society member Leonora F. Curtin launched a similar venture, The Native Market, on Palace Avenue in Santa Fe. Curtin's goal, like the society's, was to provide artists with both a sales venue and the skills to create traditional works that would prove saleable in the contemporary market. Artists were encouraged to experiment within their traditions rather than to produce mere replicas. The Native Market thus boasted a diverse, innovative array of quality works at reasonable prices. The store was moved to College Street in 1937 and continued to give Hispanic artisans an important creative and economic outlet until 1940.[6] Established artists as well as students being trained through the State Department of Vocational Education sold their works at The Native Market. Celso Gallegos and José Dolores López both exhibited santos there, as did Santa Fean Lorenzo López, whose carved burros and *carretas* with oxen were popular in a number of local curio shops. Other Native Market artists included tinsmiths Francisco Delgado and Pedro Quintana, weaver David Salazar, and furniture maker Abad Lucero, all of whom contributed significantly to the revitalization of those crafts. Traditional furniture, textiles, and tin were most frequently sold at The Native Market, but the most popular items were little wooden animals carved by Leandro Montoya. Montoya's burros, simply carved with minipiles of wood strapped to their backs, often sold on days when nothing else did and were considered the symbol of The Native Market. Three examples of Montoya's work—a St. Isidore bulto and two angel bultos—are included in the Spanish Colonial Arts Society collection. Demonstrations by artists were another major highlight of The Native Market. Weavers, tinsmiths, furniture makers, and others worked at their art while locals and tourists filed through the shop. One of those artists was Tillie Gabaldón Stark, a Santa Fe native who demonstrated her vegetal dyeing technique and *colcha* embroidery skills. Stark's efforts to preserve the distinctive *colcha* embroidery stitch, as well as natural dyeing techniques through the use of native herbs, barks, and vegetables began at The Native Market and continued until her death in 1979. Besides dyeing her own hand-spun yarns, Stark worked exclusively with traditional Spanish motifs, incorporating animals, leaves, trees, and flowers into original altar cloth designs. Her trademark signature was a morning glory flower with the name ''Tillie'' stitched delicately within. An estimated 350 native New Mexico artists earned a living through Leonora Curtin's Native Market before it closed in 1940. Meanwhile, the WPA Federal Art Project (after 1939, Federal Art Program) had been operating since 1935 under the direction of Russell Vernon Hunter. Native Market artist Eliseo Rodríguez, a painter and later a straw appliqué artist, took part in the government work-relief program.

Other Hispanic artists, among them wood-carvers Patrocinio Barela and Juan Sanchez, were identified by Hunter and hired for the project. Born in Bisbee, Arizona, in 1908, Patrocinio Barela moved to Taos when he was four.[7] Illiterate all his life, he worked as a miner, a shepherd, a migrant farm worker, and a field hand in New Mexico, Utah, and Colorado. After repairing a broken santo for a local priest in 1931, he began to carve. By 1936 Hunter had noticed his religious sculptures, prompting him to recruit Barela for the project. Barela's works were not those of the typical New Mexico santero. Carved mostly from cedar, juniper, or pine, his unpainted sculptures usually depicted biblical themes but in an original and abstract manner. Characterized by highly stylized but distorted forms, Barela's figures are known for their monumental impact in spite of their small scale. His Saint James (*Santiago*), for example, which is in the Spanish Colonial Arts Society collection, features four jumbled forms—Saint James riding his horse stoically over two Moors—all of which emerge from all sides of the squat chunk of cedar. Although simple in appearance, Barela's abstract rendition of Spain's patron saint, who appeared to Spanish soldiers during battles with the Moors, evokes the complexity and emotional power of his subject. During his years with the New Mexico Federal Art Project, Barela's talents flourished into a contemporary, sophisticated style. His carvings caught the eye of art critics nationwide, who often called him a native Henry Moore, the contemporary English sculptor. Barela's work also was compared to the primitive art of Africa and Oceania and to the carved stone figures of Easter Island. His pieces were displayed throughout the nation in Federal Art Project traveling exhibitions and eventually were added to permanent collections at New York's Museum of Modern Art and at the Baltimore Museum. Despite his fame Barela shunned the complexities of the art world. Instead, he sold his sculptures door-to-door for small amounts of cash, earning barely enough money to care for his family. He continued to carve until his tragic death in a 1964 fire, all the while breaking farther and farther away from the earlier santero tradition. Today he remains a pivotal figure in the evolution of Hispanic art and is a major influence on the work of traditional and contemporary artists alike. Another important but little-known art project artist was Juan Sanchez from the northeastern New Mexico town of Colmor.[8] His job was to reproduce traditional santos found in northern New Mexico churches for inclusion in Federal Art Project museum exhibitions. In their likeness to older traditional painted works, Sanchez's images were a sharp contrast to the more modernist works that had brought Barela national acclaim. Still, his strict adherence to traditional techniques and iconography played a major role in increasing awareness of traditional Hispanic religious art nationwide. Indeed, what distinguished Sanchez most from other Revival-period artists who worked for the project was the historical accuracy of his santos. Sanchez worked from examples of traditional bultos and retablos found in rural churches, chapels, and *moradas* throughout northern New Mexico. He sketched and carved

PATROCINIO BARELA
in his Taos studio, ca. 1950

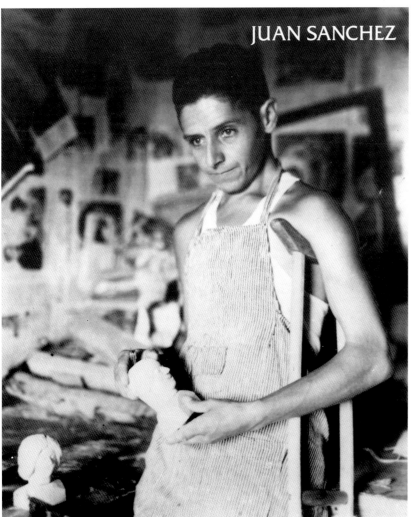

JUAN SANCHEZ

72. Patrocinio Barela, *St. James (Santiago),* ca. 1950, Taos, New Mexico. Cedar. Gift of Harold and Hilda Street.   **73.** José Mondragón, *Nativity,* 1965, Córdova, New Mexico. Cedar. Acquired at Spanish Market 1965; bequest of Alan and Ann Vedder.   **74.** Apolonio O. Martínez, *Good Shepherd,* 1971, Chimayó, New Mexico. White juniper wood. Signed and dated August 27, 1971. Awarded first prize and purchase award at Spanish Market 1971.

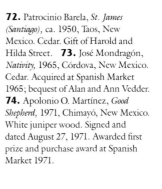

72

73

74

his own creations with amazing exactitude in materials, size, color, and proportion of the prototypes. Sanchez maintained the true beauty and spirit of the original works with only minor technical differences.

lthough devout in his religion, Sanchez viewed his work as serving a more technical than religious purpose and thus did not consider himself a "real santero." Still, he believed the cultural importance of creating religious images for display in a secular museum context to be integral to creating an awareness of faith among Hispanics and Anglos alike. His work for the project was prolific, and the historical likeness of his

77

75. Anon., Weaving, early 20th century, Mexico, probably Río de Mayo area near Navajoa, Sonora, Mexico. Wool, commercial dyes. Gift of Byron Harvey III.   **76.** Hermeregildo Jaramillo, Rio Grande blanket, ca. 1920–35, Chimayó, New Mexico. Commercial and hand-spun wool.   **77.** Anon., Hanging shelf, early 20th century, Spain. Oak, brass. Purchased in Madrid. Bequest of Alan and Ann Vedder. **78.** Mary Jane Colter, Armchair, early 20th century. Pine. Bequest of Alan and Ann Vedder. Designed for one of the Fred Harvey Company hotels.

75

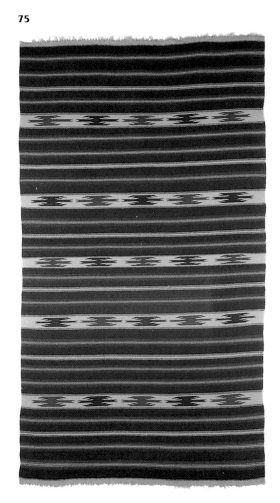

76

78

79

80

81

82

83

79. Mary Jane Colter, Side chair, ca. 1929–30. Pine. Bequest of Alan and Ann Vedder. One of a set designed for the lunchroom of Fred Harvey's hotel in Winslow, Arizona. **80.** Anon., Side chair, 20th century, New Mexico. Pine. Bequest of Alan and Ann Vedder. **81.** Anon., Side chair, 20th century, New Mexico. Pine. Bequest of Alan and Ann Vedder. **82.** Anon., Table, 20th century, New Mexico. Pine. Bequest of Alan and Ann Vedder. **83.** William Penhallow Henderson, Table, 1930s, Santa Fe, New Mexico. Wood. Bequest of Alan and Ann Vedder.

santos remained key to his art in later years. The artist continued to make santos for collectors and tourists until his death in 1969.

Sanchez's work is included in collections at the Palace of the Governors, the Museum of International Folk Art, the Taylor Museum of the Colorado Springs Fine Arts Center, and the Colorado Collection at the University of Colorado in Boulder. It plays an important role in preserving the aesthetic integrity of traditional colonial santos and serves as an invaluable cultural bridge between traditional santero art in the colonial period, the Revival period, and today. Throughout the early, prewar Revival period of Hispanic arts, Anglo patrons exercised a strong influence on native artists, directly and indirectly encouraging variations in their styles in an attempt to make the work more marketable to new buyers. As Hispanic artists had done throughout the colonial period and the nineteenth century, they continued to adapt to technological change and new materials and tools, but they no longer created religious or utilitarian objects solely for their own Hispanic communities. Now objects were being purchased by a generally wealthy, usually Protestant and predominantly Anglo clientele. Religious images became decorative curiosities in Anglo homes, unpainted images replaced painted ones, secular images increased, and new forms as record album holders and lazy Susans were introduced. Traditional tin boxes now had slits in the top for dispensing tissues and tin sconces were wired for electricity. Unfortunately it is impossible to know precisely to what extent the new market and the mentors affected the work of individual artists or whether and to what extent the artists followed their own inclinations. The term revival may not be the most appropriate, since it is obvious that some Hispanic art forms continued to be produced at least on a small scale within many communities during the early decades of the twentieth century. Nonetheless, the new patronage inspired a resurgence and, in many cases, a stylistic redirection of these arts. The so-called revival of traditional Hispanic arts had reached its peak by the 1930s and soon was eclipsed by World War II. During the early 1950s it was clear that support for the revitalization of traditional Hispanic arts in northern New Mexico had not been lost during the war. Artists who had made significant contributions to the prewar movement were still practicing their respective arts after the war and still passing them on to successive generations. Former New Mexico Federal Art Project worker E. Boyd led a successful effort to reorganize the Spanish Colonial Arts Society in 1952. Boyd, who was the first curator of Spanish colonial art at the Museum of New Mexico, also had a hand in encouraging other artists to pursue traditional art work. When Santa Fe santero Max Roybal informed Boyd that he had decided to stop making santos, she persuaded him otherwise by convincing him of the need to perpetuate such arts.[9] Roybal, who went on to teach wood carving at the University of New Mexico and at area high schools, continued to practice his art in Albuquerque until his death in 1995. In 1959 José Mondragón joined the Córdova carving tradition after a hunting accident prevented him from continuing

84

85

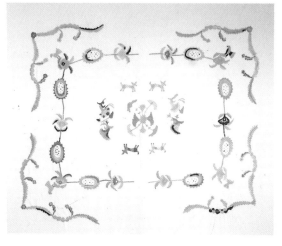

86

84. Policarpio Valencia, Embroidery, early 20th century, Santa Cruz, New Mexico. Commercial wool and cotton cloth, dyed cotton string. **85.** Rebecca Salsbury James, *Christ Child of Atocha*, 1960–61, Taos, New Mexico. *Colcha* embroidery: linen, commercial wool yarn, metallic thread. Gift of artist. **86.** Nellie Dunton, Bedspread, ca. 1929–33, New Mexico. *Colcha* embroidery: linen, wool yarn. Gift of Lois Field.

his work as a rancher.[10] Although not related to the renowned López family, Mondragón's refined simplicity and precise techniques echoed their style. Prior to his death in 1990, he carved his pine or cottonwood pieces with a pocketknife, embellishing them with filigree designs instead of paint. His wife, Alice Mondragón, was a partner in his work, and the two also are noted for their straw appliqué crosses and unusual wooden rosaries. One of Mondragón's pieces, a Córdova style *nacimiento,* is included in the Spanish Colonial Arts Society collection.

The early 1960s brought notice to Sigfried Martínez and Apolonio Martínez, Chimayó wood-carvers whose unpainted works also reveal the influence of their Córdova neighbors.[11] Apolonio Martínez, a carpenter, began to carve santos in 1964 following his retirement at seventy-two. Although unpainted, Martínez's images differ stylistically from the Córdova tradition in his more naturalistic approach. Often using multitoned aspen, his work is slightly rough in texture. Instead of employing incised surface ornamentation to emphasize specific features of his work, Martínez's images emerge subtly from a smooth wood surface. With the encouragement of E. Boyd and others, Apolonio Martínez continued to carve until his death in 1976. In the years leading up to and following World War II, the activities of the Spanish Colonial Arts Society were sporadic. Spanish markets were held irregularly in the 1920s and 1930s, then they lapsed entirely. In 1965 the reorganized society sponsored on the Santa Fe plaza its first Spanish Market, and it proved to be a major vehicle in the society's continued mission to provide an artistically and economically viable outlet for native Hispanic artists. It also inspired the more recent revival of traditional Hispanic art forms during the last three decades among a growing number of artists throughout the region.

87. Probably by Tillie Gabaldón Stark, *Colcha* embroidery, ca. 1930–49, New Mexico. Cotton twill, wool yarn, commercial dyes. Gift of Cornelia G. Thompson.

NOTES

1. See chapter 2.

2. To date no definitive work has been published on Celso Gallegos. The following sources were used here: unpublished files and accession records, Spanish Colonial Arts Society (hereafter SCAS); vertical file on Celso Gallegos, Library of the Museum of International Folk Art (hereafter MOIFA), Santa Fe; "Celso Gallegos, Fabricador de los Santos de Bulto," *El Pasatiempo,* 5 September 1931, 9. See also Carmella M. Padilla, "Celso Gallegos," *El Palacio* 99, 3 (Summer 1994): 22–27, 57.

3. Unpublished files and accession records, SCAS; vertical files, MOIFA Library; E. Boyd, *Popular Arts of Spanish New Mexico* (Santa Fe: Museum of New Mexico Press, 1974), 265, 468–71; Charles L. Briggs, "To Talk in Different Tongues: The 'Discovery' and 'Encouragement' of Hispano Woodcarvers by Santa Fe Patrons, 1919–1945," in William Wroth, ed., *Hispanic Crafts of the Southwest* (Colorado Springs: Taylor Museum of the Colorado Springs Fine Arts

Center, 1977), 37–51. Also see Charles L. Briggs, *The Wood Carvers of Córdova, New Mexico: Social Dimensions of an Artistic "Revival"* (Knoxville: University of Tennessee Press, 1980).

4. This image is in the collection of the Taylor Museum of the Colorado Springs Fine Arts Center in Colorado Springs, Colorado. For a reproduction see Briggs, *Wood Carvers,* pl. 11.

5. Marta Weigle, "The First Twenty-Five Years of the Spanish Colonial Arts Society," in Weigle with Claudia Larcombe and Samuel Larcombe, eds., *Hispanic Arts and Ethnohistory in the Southwest: New Papers Inspired by the Work of E. Boyd* (Santa Fe: Ancient City Press; Albuquerque: University of New Mexico Press, 1983), 188–92; and chapter 2.

6. Sarah Nestor, *The Native Market of the Spanish New Mexican Craftsmen, Santa Fe, 1933–1940* (Santa Fe: The Colonial New Mexico Historical Foundation, 1978); and chapter 1.

7. This section is based on unpublished files and accession records, SCAS; vertical files, MOIFA

Library; Briggs, *Wood Carvers,* 86–88; Wroth, *Hispanic Crafts,* 99. Also see Mildred Crews, Wendell Anderson and Judson Crews, *Patrocinio Barela: Taos Woodcarver* (Taos, N.M.: Taos Recordings and Publications, 1962); Mildred Crews, "Patrocinio Barela: Woodcarver of Taos," *Presbyterian Life,* 15 February 1968, 7–11; Vernon Hunter, "Concerning Patrocinio Barela," in Francis V. O'Connor, ed., *Art for the Millions: Essays from the 1930s by Artists and Administrators of the WPA Federal Art Project* (Boston: New York Graphic Society, 1973), 96–99.

8. To date no definitive work on Sanchez has been published. This section is based on Thomas L. Reidel, "Copied for the W.P.A.: Juan A. Sanchez, American Tradition and The New Deal Politics of Saint-Making" (M.A. thesis, University of Colorado, 1992).

9. Claudia Larcombe, "E. Boyd: A Biographical Sketch," in *Hispanic Arts,* 9.

10. Briggs, *Wood Carvers;* SCAS; MOIFA.

11. Ibid.

4. The Revival of Straw Appliqué and Tinwork

Perhaps the most mysterious of all Spanish colonial arts is straw appliqué, whose origins are shrouded in speculation at times as wonderful as the art form itself.[1] E. Boyd observes that "in combinations of tiny particles of straw the variations of yellow produce a golden glitter which satisfactorily resembles gold leaf, literally poor man's gilding."[2] Straw appliqué is still described as "poor man's gold" by the handful of artists who practice it today. The twentieth-century revival of straw appliqué is largely credited to one man, Eliseo Rodríguez. He was born on September 21, 1915, and until 1929, had lived a "pretty nice" life.[3] The Great Depression affected everyone in Santa Fe, and for those who could not retreat to farmland, life became "rough and tumble." With the economy still tenuous in 1935, Rodríguez nonetheless decided to marry his childhood sweetheart Paula Gutiérrez. By 1936 the Federal Art Project had begun in New Mexico, and local artists were able to make seventy-nine dollars a month teaching and producing art. Rodríguez soon joined this work-relief program as a painter. WPA director Russell Vernon Hunter had once seen a straw or cornhusk appliqué cross. At Hunter's suggestion Rodríguez "was given a chance to revive the whole field." As he says: "It was exciting and a challenge. We had no method of working so we made it up as we went along." His educated guesses about appliqué materials and processes were based on other art forms such as furniture, retablos, and bultos. In older pieces seasoned pine or cottonwood was hand-adzed to form the crosses.[4] If prepared further the wood received one or several coats of *yeso* (gesso) made from local gypsum rock that was baked, pulverized, dissolved in water, and then mixed with animal glue. At times a wash of egg or glue with water was applied as a final preparation. To make black paint, pine sap dissolved in grain alcohol (*trementina*) was mixed with *hollín* (lampblack) or *tisne* (charcoal). The less common blue and red crosses were made with indigo and mercuric sulfide, respectively, both imports from Old Mexico. Pieces of wheat straw were then split down, flattened, and scraped with the knife blade to bring out their luster. They were then cut into geometric shapes according to the design that the artist had in mind. A more viscous *trementina* was used as the gluing agent.[5] Finally, the completed crosses received an additional coat of *trementina*. Having worked with an array of media, Eliseo Rodríguez found that it was "mosaics that were the connection to design." Also a painter, he used those skills to create subtly shaded straw appliqué by manipulating the varying degrees of color in the straw to portray saints and religious scenes.[6] His working knowledge of oil paints, acrylics, and lithography imbued his work with a painterly quality. Eliseo Rodríguez recalls: "We were young. We experimented. My first piece was actually inlaid rather than applied." The "we" in his history is *"mi hija"* (my daughter), his affectionate name for his wife Paula. "Paula has been making the crosses continuously since 1936. The war interrupted my own growth." The straw appliqué of wife Paula, daughter Vicki, and four grandchildren Marcial, Gabriel, Jessica, and Monica clearly expresses the family's love for this unique art form. Failing eyesight has affected both Eliseo and Paula, but as of this writing Eliseo is once again at work creating an eight-foot cross after a respite of three years. Another family carrying the tradition of straw appliqué to new levels of artistry includes Jimmy and Debbie Trujillo and their children Jaime and Cordilia. A purist in tradition, Jimmy began making straw appliqué crosses in 1984 after being inspired by the work of his compadre Charles Carrillo and by the crosses in the Abiquiú *morada* where both men are *hermanos* (brothers). Carrillo has said of Trujillo's work, "I gave him the recipe, but he's the one who has baked the cake!" The traditional processes employed by the Trujillo family render their crosses clearly distinctive and magnificent. Other notable Hispanic artists perpetuating the labor-intensive art form inspired by the Rodríguez and Trujillo families are Felix López and his daughter Krissa. Known for his exquisite and elegant bultos, López saw his first straw appliqué cross at the Museum of International Folk Art in 1977. Fascinated by the "humble materials" with their enormous spiritual impact, he went home and immediately searched the family barn in Santa Cruz for wheat straw. Creating a black cross similar to what he had seen and liked "because of the beautiful contrast of gold on black," he began arranging patterns with straw and, in effect, taught himself the art form. His first cross was purchased the following summer at Spanish Market by Alan C. Vedder and is now in the collection of the Spanish Colonial Arts Society. Straw appliqué also continues to a very limited extent among some Pueblo Indian communities in New Mexico. Leo Coriz, an eighty-year-old Santo Domingo resident, recalls his family and friends making religious and decorative items when he was a child. "It was often that I saw the straw in the church and in the homes." Boyd notes that "only one or two Indians of Santa Ana Pueblo have continued with the work [of straw appliqué], but their sense of design makes it most attractive."[7] During August's annual Indian Market in Santa Fe, straw appliqué artist Elmer Leon from Santa Ana Pueblo usually displays his work.

88. Paula Rodríguez, Straw appliqué
cross, 1981, Santa Fe, New Mexico.
Pine, paint, straw. Bequest of Alan and
Ann Vedder.   **89.** Eliseo Rodríguez,
Straw appliqué cross, 1978, Santa Fe,
New Mexico. Pine, paint, straw.

88

89

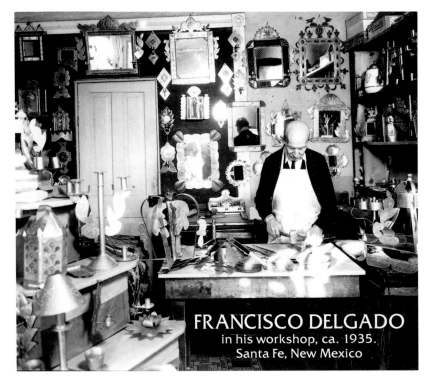

FRANCISCO DELGADO
in his workshop, ca. 1935.
Santa Fe, New Mexico

The 1930s also saw the revival of "poor man's silver," the tin art, much of it religious, that began to flourish after the United States Army occupied New Mexico in 1846.[8] The appearance of imported tin cans coupled with Bishop Lamy's 1850 appointment to New Mexico in part caused certain forms of local religious art, such as retablos, to fall out of fashion while European prints framed in tin came into vogue. Until 1890, when commercial picture frames began to replace tin frames and coal and gas lighting replaced the need for candle holders, tin artists provided art made for pennies that today sells for thousands. Lane Coulter and Maurice Dixon, Jr., claim that "the New Mexican production of tinwork primarily for religious purposes is unparalleled elsewhere in American folk arts."[9] The most abundant forms were tin frames for religious prints and sometimes mirrors and niches created to protect bultos as they simultaneously provided a shrine for the home. Small chests (*baulitos*) or boxes (*cajitas*) were often made for religious use as reliquaries (*relicarios*), although some evidence exists to suggest their use for holding private articles. Other tin objects for religious use include Host boxes, tin crowns for bultos, and three-part processional sets consisting of a cross on a stave with two long torches. Although some purely utilitarian, nonreligious items, such as buckets, cups, and shelves (*repisas*), have been found, they are not numerous and rarely if ever the primary focus of the tin artist. Coulter and Dixon have identified thirteen workshops representing about twenty-five Hispanic New Mexican and Mexican craftsmen in five counties who produced 90 percent of the tin art in nineteenth-century New Mexico.[10] These were the artists who inspired the Revival artists of the twentieth century when mass production, coal, gas, and other modern conveniences and attitudes contributed to the decline of tin products.

Both the Spanish Colonial Arts Society and Leonora F. Curtin's Native Market helped stem this decline. The latter provided venue for a resident tin artist, Pedro Quintana. Unlike previous tinwork produced for religious purposes, Revival pieces were designed for secular use in a modern world: frames for mirrors, electrified home fixtures, tissue boxes, and ashtrays. No longer made from tin obtained from tin cans, modern pieces were made from sheets of terneplate, a darker-toned material that imitates the look of the now older New Mexican pieces. Local vocational schools also provided a catalyst for the revival of tinwork. To help students, Carmen Espinosa wrote *New Mexico Tincraft*, published by the State Department of Vocational Education in 1937. The book contains drawings of several early tin pieces and became a source of inspiration for Revival-period tin artists. According to Coulter and Dixon, "besides the popular Santa Fe Federal Style, the workshops most often used as a design source by Revival tinsmiths were the Valencia Red and Green, Valencia Red and Green II, Rio Arriba Painted, and Mora Octagonal. . . . [However, a] discussion of the work of the most notable Revival tinsmiths will show that while many nineteenth-century motifs were utilized, the major tinsmiths did develop work of individual character nevertheless."[11] Among the Revival artists—all Santa Feans—are Francisco Sandoval (1860–1944), Francisco Delgado (1858–1936), his son Ildeberto (Eddie) Delgado (1883–1966), Benjamin Sweringen (active 1928–36), Pedro Quintana (1910–1988?), Robert Woodman (1908–1983), and Bruce Cooper (1905–1987). Today's tin artists, notably Angelina Delgado and her protégé Fred Ray López, the Romero family, and Bonifacio Sandoval, expertly continue an art form that gives only what is necessary to modernization.[12] "Poor man's silver" is still made more or less as it was a century and a half ago.

90. Francisco Sandoval, Sconce (one of pair), ca. 1939, Santa Fe, New Mexico. Terneplate, mirror glass. Commissioned from artist by Cady Wells. Bequest of Cady Wells. **91.** Anon., Frame, early 20th century, New Mexico. Terneplate, paper, paint, mirror glass. Bequest of Alan and Ann Vedder. **92.** José María Apodaca, Sconce (one of pair), ca. 1900, Santa Fe, New Mexico. Tinplate, wallpaper, glass. Bequest of Alan and Ann Vedder. **93.** Possibly by Bruce Cooper or Benjamin Sweringen, Frame, 1928–36, Santa Fe, New Mexico. Terneplate, paint, mirror glass. Originally collected from the Spanish Chest owned by Sweringen. Bequest of Alan and Ann Vedder.

90

91

92

93

NOTES

1. For a discussion of the history of straw appliqué see Donna Pierce and Marta Weigle, eds., *Spanish New Mexico: The Collection of the Spanish Colonial Arts Society,* 2 vols. (Santa Fe: Museum of New Mexico Press, 1996), vol. 1, chap. 5.

2. E. Boyd, *Popular Arts of Spanish New Mexico* (Santa Fe: Museum of New Mexico Press, 1974), 309–10.

3. The following is based on a personal interview with Eliseo Rodríguez, September 1993.

4. This discussion of technique of manufacture is based on Roland F. Dickey, *New Mexico Village Arts,* (1949; reprint, Albuquerque: University of New Mexico, 1970), 65, 69–71; and independent research performed by santero Charles Carrillo, personal communication, September 1993.

5. Today some artists opt for commercial wood glues, arguing that they give a better archival quality.

6. In 1985 Eliseo Rodríguez was honored for his excellence in painting. He was one of only twenty artists selected for sidewalk plaques in front of the Museum of New Mexico's Fine Arts Museum in Santa Fe.

7. Boyd, *Popular Arts,* 310.

8. See Pierce and Weigle, *Spanish New Mexico,* vol. 1, chap. 7.

9. Lane Coulter and Maurice Dixon, Jr., *Tinwork in New Mexico, 1840–1940* (Albuquerque: University of New Mexico Press, 1990), 17.

10. For a detailed discussion of these workshops, see Pierce and Weigle, *Spanish New Mexico,* vol. 1, chap. 7.

11. Coulter and Dixon, *Tinwork,* 143–44.

12. For more on contemporary tin artists see chapters 5 and 6.

5. Spanish Market

Color photographs of Spanish Market from 1975 to 1995 by Jack Parsons; black-and-white photographs by Nancy Hunter Warren.

In 1965 the Spanish Colonial Arts Society revived Spanish Market, which it originally had sponsored from 1926 until the mid-1930s. Held in conjunction with the annual Indian Market on the Santa Fe plaza, it renewed the society's commitment to support the artistic growth of Hispanic artists native to New Mexico and southern Colorado and working in traditional art forms. Spanish Market remained part of Indian Market until 1972, when the event took its own place on the plaza during the last full weekend of July. A smaller Winter Market, started by the society in 1989, is held in downtown Santa Fe each December. Today, after two decades of marked growth and change, the once-intimate Spanish Market has become the largest exhibition of traditional Hispanic arts in the United States. The society honors artistic excellence at the July Spanish Market by purchasing outstanding works of art for its collection and by awarding prizes. Its grand prize, first prize, and other special awards recognize distinctive skill and innovation in various media. These awards, funded by the society and private contributions, are determined each year by an independent panel of judges. Special annual awards recognize valuable contributions to the society's work. The E. Boyd Memorial Award for originality and expressive design was established in 1979 in honor of Boyd, a former society curator and longtime staunch supporter of traditional Hispanic arts. The Alan and Ann Vedder Memorial Award for proficiency in the use of traditional materials and techniques, begun in 1990, recognizes the tireless work of Alan Vedder, who replaced Boyd as society curator in 1965, and his wife, Ann, in their efforts to expand and preserve the society's collection. The International Folk Art Foundation inaugurated the Florence Dibbell Bartlett Award for innovative design in 1986 to honor the founder of the Museum of International Folk Art. Among other annual special prizes is the Bienvenidos Award for a first-time market exhibitor who shows exceptional promise. The Hispanic Heritage Award, also sponsored by the International Folk Art Foundation, applauds an artist for in-depth research of historical techniques and iconography. The Archbishop's Award, sponsored by the Archdiocese of Santa Fe, recognizes art that portrays a religious theme in a traditional New Mexico

CARMELLA PADILLA

52

style. Finally, the Master's Award for Lifetime Achievement goes to an artist whose work through the years has greatly contributed to sustaining a given art form and increasing knowledge about traditional Hispanic art in general. A review of work by prizewinning artists between 1965 and 1994 gives valuable insight into the twentieth-century evolution of traditional Hispanic arts and artists. By breaking new ground while working within the context of an established tradition, these artists ensure a lasting place for that tradition in contemporary culture. Although it is impossible to mention every participating or award-winning artist in Spanish Market history, those who have earned grand or first prizes and occasional special awards are mentioned. Many of these artists also have work in the Spanish Colonial Arts Society collection. Because unpublished records and files of the Spanish Colonial Arts Society are sketchy and erratic about prizewinners between 1966 and 1977, this period may be incompletely documented. Eighteen exhibitors attended the 1965 Spanish Market, which was held on the plaza's west end under the portal of the First National Bank of Santa Fe. Tesuque wood-carver Ben Ortega was awarded the grand

prize for his distinctive driftwood, cedar, and cottonwood carvings of Saint Francis of Assisi, other religious images, and birds and animals. Córdova's George López, whose works spanned the transition from the 1920s Revival period to the post-war revival, shared the first place award for wood carving with José Mondragón, also of Córdova. Tillie Gabaldón Stark of Santa Fe, whose efforts to maintain the *colcha* embroidery tradition began at The Native Market in the 1930s, won first prize in that category. Weaver Felix Ortega, tinworker Conchita Quintana, and silversmith Andy Rivera, Jr., all took first place in their respective categories. A scheduling problem caused the cancellation of the 1966 Spanish Market, but it was resumed in 1967 and thereafter took place on an annual basis. By 1971 the increased number of participating artists required its relocation to the portal of the Palace of the Governors. It was the last year Spanish Market would be held in conjunction with Indian Market. Prizewinners during the late 1960s and early 1970s are not systematically recorded in society papers, but various artists who later won prizes entered the market during that time. Taos santero Leo Salazar began exhibiting at Spanish Market in the early 1970s. He began carving as a young man with the encouragement and assistance of his uncle, renowned Revival-period Taos wood-carver Patrocinio Barela. Using a chisel his uncle had given him, Salazar echoed Barela in his early work but soon developed his own unique style. Using cedar that had been cured for at least three years, Salazar stressed the natural qualities of the wood. His diverse religious subjects, including images from both the Old and New Testaments, were generally made from a single piece of wood and thus were no larger than the cedar stumps and limbs the artist collected from nearby mountains. Instead of paint, Salazar highlighted the natural textures and colors of the wood. In his *Moses,* for example, the image emerges from a single piece of wood. The artist takes advantage of the natural white outer edge of the red cedar log to contrast the figure's beard from the rest of his body. Likewise, in *San Miguel and Demon* Salazar brilliantly uses the natural wood grain to give the piece its magnificent contrast and depth. Leo Salazar was a regular Spanish Market exhibitor and award-winner until his death in 1990. His sons, Ernesto, Leonardo, and Ricardo, have followed their father as Spanish Market artists working in his distinctive unpainted carving style. Shortly before he died he received the Master's Award for Lifetime Achievement. The early 1970s also marked the entrance of another first family of traditional art to Spanish Market. Santa Fe tinworkers Emilio and Senaida Romero, who had been creating traditional decorative, devotional, and

utilitarian works in tin since the late 1950s, became regular participants at that time. During the next two decades they won numerous first-place and special awards, including many for Senaida for *colcha* embroidery. Many of the Romeros's children, grandchildren, and great-grandchildren have since followed in their footsteps as Spanish Market exhibitors in a variety of media. Members of the renowned López family emerged in the early 1970s as the new generation of Córdova carvers. José Dolores López's grandchildren, Gloria López Córdova and Eluid Martínez, and other relatives continued the family tradition of chip-carving ornate filigree designs onto unpainted wood. In its strict adherence to the traditional Córdova technique and motifs, their work represents the successful transition of the family style from the early to the late twentieth century. Gloria López Córdova won first prize in the bulto category in 1979 and 1980. Chimayó wood-carver Apolonio

Martínez first exhibited at Spanish Market in 1971. Then eighty, Martínez was said to have stayed up an entire Friday night to complete a bulto by the next day. The piece, *El Buen Pastor,* took first place in the wood-carving category and was purchased for the society's collection. In 1972, Nambé santero Orlando Romero made his Spanish Market debut with an array of painted and unpainted wood carvings. The abstract style of many of Romero's works reveals the influence of Revival-era artist Patrocinio Barela. In Romero's unpainted *San Cristobal,* in the society's collection, an abstract image of Saint Christopher carrying the baby Jesus on his back emerges from a gnarled block of wood, recalling Barela's 1950 *Santiago* (St. James) in composition and style. *Maria and Popovi Da,* purchased for the society's collection in 1974, is a departure from more traditional themes. The piece features an abstract depiction of San Ildefonso potter Maria Martínez with her newborn son, Popovi Da, and is finished in a highly polished matte black. Two other works by Romero, *Holy Family* and *David and Goliath,* are also in the society's collection. As a participant of the market until 1981, Romero earned first prize and other awards for his innovative wood carvings. Prompted by a series of workshops in the mid-1970s and encouragement from E. Boyd and Alan Vedder, some Hispanic artists researched artifact collections for inspiration and historical accuracy. Such research into traditional arts resulted in the addition of several categories to the 1975 Spanish Market: furniture, straw appliqué, and filigree jewelry. Española's Derek Sandoval de la Cruz, one of few artists making traditional filigree jewelry at the time, had begun his interest in jewelry-making as a teenager. He later learned the art of filigree by studying old pieces made by his great-grandfather, Desiderio Sandoval. Working in both gold and silver, Sandoval won first prize for filigree in 1975. Prize winners in the 1975 wood-carving category reflected an important transition in that medium from the Revival era to the present. While George López, Apolonio Martínez, and Agua Fria wood-carver M. A. Chávez represented the unpainted carving style made popular by the Córdova carvers, the work of Santa Fe santero Luis Tapia at once marked a return to and a departure from the polychromed images of the eighteenth and nineteenth centuries. Tapia, who began participating in market during the early 1970s, made bold use of homemade gesso and egg tempera paints for a new expression in the traditional art. He later used commercial gesso and acrylics

54

to create his innovative and modern interpretations of traditional santero art. A multitalented artist, Tapia took first prize in the wood-carving category as well as first and second prizes in the furniture category in 1975, the first year that furniture became a market category. He received first prize in furniture again in 1977 and 1978. The early 1970s also marked the market debut of another santero whose exquisitely painted wood carvings earned him wide acclaim. Horacio Valdez of Dixon developed a unique style of bultos and retablos that echoed traditional polychromed images. His highly refined carving abilities combined with a brilliant use of acrylics defined a distinctive place for him among contemporary santeros. Along with Tapia, Valdez's presence at Spanish Market inspired a revival of painted santos. Valdez exhibited there for more than ten years, winning numerous honors, including first prize in the bulto category in 1985. In 1992, one month before his death, Valdez returned to Spanish Market and was honored with a special exhibition of his work. Most 1975 first-prize winners adhered to tradition. Maria T. Lujan of Española, first-prize winner in the *colcha* embroidery category in 1975, 1977, 1979, and 1982, was a co-founder in 1932 of Arte Antigua, an organization devoted to reviving the traditional *colcha* embroidery style. Her significant contributions to the preservation of the art were acknowledged by the grand-prize award in 1980. Likewise, Santa Fe's Efren Martínez and his wife, Angelina Delgado Martínez, first- and second-prize winners, respectively, represented the family tin-working tradition established by her grandfather, Francisco Delgado, and her father, Ildeberto (Eddie) Delgado. In the intervening years, Angelina has received first-place honors six times and a Master's Award for Lifetime Achievement in 1991. Maria Vergara Wilson of Albuquerque, winner of the 1977 grand and first prizes for weaving, also returned to tradition for weaving techniques. Her use of natural dyes and her revival of the historic ikat weaving method were based on historical research. Instructed in the art by renowned Medanales weaver Cordelia Coronado, Wilson is proficient in the Rio Grande weaving styles of traditional *jerga,* Saltillo, and Vallero and in *colcha* embroidery techniques. Wilson's versatile talents were honored with first prizes for *jerga* in 1983 and *colcha* embroidery in 1984. Anita Romero Jones of Santa Fe, who learned the art of tinwork from her parents, Emilio and Senaida Romero, made her Spanish Market debut

in 1977. Romero Jones demonstrated her artistic versatility with a first prize in the retablo category in 1977 and 1984, in the bulto category in 1978, and a grand prize plus a first prize for tinwork in 1985. In 1989 she also received the Hispanic Heritage Award for her in-depth research on a bulto of Our Lady of Guadalupe. Despite a hearty showing by a new generation of traditional Hispanic artists at the 1977 Spanish Market, the first-prize win by Max Roybal of Albuquerque in the bulto category represented the continued contributions of longtime market artists. Spanish Market of 1978 marked the entrance of two more extraordinary young Artists: Española weaver Teresa Archuleta-Sagel and La Cienega furniture-maker David C de Baca. Archuleta-Sagel brought a new dimension to the Rio Grande weaving tradition with her innovative designs and use of traditional materials. She received two market awards that year—the grand prize and the first-prize award for weaving—and would continue to win top weaving awards until her last Spanish Market exhibition in 1985. C de Baca's close attention to traditional Spanish colonial furniture techniques earned him a second-place award in the furniture category that year. One year later, he had refined his skills to take both the grand prize and the first prize for furniture. C de Baca continued to take home top awards thereafter. Santa Feans Star Tapia and Juan Jimenez received first-place awards in the straw appliqué and retablo divisions, respectively, in 1978 and again in 1979. Jimenez took another first in his category in 1981. In spite of the strong showing by young artists, established embroiderer Tillie Gabaldón Stark and tinworkers Emilio and Senaida Romero retained first prizes in their categories in 1978. With the beginning of the new decade the society made a commitment to purchase more contemporary artworks to round out its twentieth-century collection, giving added recognition and support for veteran and novice artists alike. By 1980 the artistry of Santa Fe santera Marie Romero Cash brought her Spanish Market recognition as a maker of traditional retablos, bultos, and tin. The daughter of tinworkers Emilio and Senaida Romero, Cash contributed to the prestigious family tradition of producing award-winning work. Her impressive list of awards through the years includes first prizes in the retablo category in 1980, 1982, 1983, 1985, 1987, and 1988 and in mixed media in 1991. Cash also received the E. Boyd Memorial Award in 1985, the Florence Dibbell Bartlett Award in 1990 and 1993, and a

Master's Award for Lifetime Achievement in 1992. The 1980 market brought attention to artists in some of the lesser-known arts. Star Tapia (now Sanchez) continued to exhibit the skill that earned her several first-place awards in the straw appliqué category. However, she is perhaps best noted for her revival of the traditional rawhide *petaca,* or traveling trunk. Blacksmith Rolando De Leon of Santa Fe won the first of many awards in the new metalworking category, now separated from tinwork, for his contributions in furthering the Hispanic ironworking tradition. One of the few artists to produce the utilitarian and decorative wares that distinguished the Spanish Colonial style, De Leon taught, demonstrated, and exhibited his skills nationwide until his death in 1989. In 1980, 1982, and 1987 Chimayó wood-carver Marco Oviedo received the E. Boyd Memorial Award for the originality and expressive design that characterize his work. One of his most historic pieces, a pine *matraca,* or traditional Penitente noisemaker, is included in the society's collection. Oviedo and his wife, Patricia, who often assists him in his work, took first place in the bulto category in 1989. Patricia is a seventh-generation member of the acclaimed Ortega and Trujillo weaving families of Chimayó. Pedro Rodríguez was awarded first place in the weaving category in 1980. Norma Maestas and Maria Hesch took top honors in weaving and *colcha,* respectively, the following year. Former Native Market and New Mexico Federal Art Project artist Eliseo Rodríguez of Santa Fe swept the 1981 Spanish Market with a number of honors, including the prestigious grand-prize award, which recognized his persistence and innovation in reviving the ancient art of straw appliqué. Rodríguez's work not only inspired later generations to practice the complex art but also led his wife Paula, daughters Vicki Rodríguez and Yolanda Griego, and many grandchildren into their own noteworthy careers as straw appliqué artists and award-winning Spanish Market participants. Paula Rodríguez took successive first-place awards in straw in 1982, 1983, 1984, and 1985. In 1989 Eliseo and Paula Rodríguez both received the Master's Award for Lifetime Achievement. During the 1980s and early 1990s, the historical research initiated in the mid-1970s became more serious and extensive. Taking advantage of museum collections for study, Hispanic artists began to look back beyond the Revival-period styles in a return to the older techniques and prototypes of the eighteenth and nineteenth

centuries. Many bulto and retablo artists began to eschew acrylics in favor of homemade vegetal and mineral paints and gesso in the colonial and nineteenth-century tradition. Some furniture makers revived the traditional use of hand-hewn and hand-adzed boards for the construction of their pieces. The early 1980s saw the emerging talents of three young santeros who would become noted for their serious research into historic methods and refined application of traditional materials: Charles Carrillo, Felix López, and Ramón José López. Carrillo, of Santa Fe, first entered Spanish Market in 1978 and began creating everything from hand-adzed retablos to gesso-relief panels and hollow-frame bultos in the style of the nineteenth-century santeros. La Mesilla artist Felix López began his market career in 1977, exhibiting unpainted santos and straw appliqué before turning his attention to skillfully carved bultos painted in colors created from natural pigments. Santa Fean Ramón José López first brought his work to market in 1981 and combined his skills as a jeweler, silversmith, and santero to become known for his fine painting and carving, as well as his innovation within traditional Spanish colonial styles. In the course of nearly two decades these three contemporary masters of traditional santero art would achieve widespread recognition with numerous grand prizes, first prizes, and special awards at Spanish Market. A special children's category was added to Spanish Market in 1981. Eleven children of established market artists proudly exhibited that year alongside their parents or other relatives. By 1994 eighty children participated in Spanish Market. Further testament to the beauty of art as a family tradition came in 1982 when Chimayó weaver Jacobo Trujillo shared Spanish Market honors with his son, weaver Irvin Trujillo. The elder Trujillo, a sixth-generation descendant of the renowned Chimayó Ortega and Trujillo weaving families, was a well-known teacher in the 1930s State Department of Vocational Education traditional arts training programs. At home on the family's Centinela Ranch Trujillo worked at a loom he built in 1927, creating some of the most versatile and intricately designed weavings of his time. His highly refined expressions of the Rio Grande weaving style earned him the Spanish Market grand prize in 1982, as well as first prize in the weaving category in 1983 and 1986. Before his death in 1990, Jacobo Trujillo was firmly established as a master of the traditional weaving style, a tradition he taught to his children. Learning to weave at his father's massive loom from the time he was ten, Irvin Trujillo quickly picked up on Jacobo's meticulous technique and imaginative use of the traditional style. The seventh-generation weaver then took the tradition one step further to create his own one-of-a-kind weavings in bright, contemporary colors and designs. Both Irvin and his wife, weaver Lisa Trujillo, have followed in the footsteps of his father as regular Spanish Market exhibitors and award-winning artists. Each has earned several first-place honors, as well as grand prizes for Irvin in 1984 and 1991. **T**he 1982 Spanish Market also brought recognition to two talented, established Santa Fe artists: Frank Brito and Monica Sosaya Halford. Longtime santero Brito, who turned to carving in 1967 after an illness brought his work as a plumber to an end, demonstrated his mastery of the art with a first-place win in the bulto category. The self-taught artist's refined images of animals and saints are carved in pine with pocketknives and hand chisels, then painted in deep, solid shades of color. The versatile Santa Fe santera Monica Sosaya Halford entered the market in 1979 and won a first prize for a door she decorated with images of saints. In 1982,

Sosaya Halford introduced glass painting as a new market category. A prolific artist, she is perhaps best known for her prodigious skills as a painter of retablos and for her fine *colcha* embroidery work, both of which have brought her several awards through the years, including the Florence Dibbell Bartlett Award for innovative design in 1987 and 1988 and the Master's Award for Lifetime Achievement in 1994. Daniel Blea of Albuquerque, who took first place in the furniture category in 1982, would later bring his talents as a bulto and retablo maker to the market in the 1990s. **B**y 1983 the brief but brilliant career of Santa Fe santero and furniture-maker John Gonzales was starting to shine as he took first- and second-place honors in furniture and third in the retablo category. Gonzales, whose works are noted for their close attention to traditional detail and style, viewed his art as a means for passing on his heritage to others. A regular Spanish Market participant with works included in major galleries nationwide, Gonzales died in 1992 having accomplished his goal. **T**he distinctive works of newcomer Tomás L. Sena were noted in 1984 with a first-place award in the santo and bulto category. Having just taken up wood carving in 1980 after a long and distinguished career with the New Mexico Department of Game and Fish, Sena quickly demonstrated his natural affinity for the art. Carving mostly cottonwood or driftwood, Sena's crude style echoes that of Revival-era santero Celso Gallegos. Sena, who lives in Glorieta, received the Master's Award for Lifetime Achievement in 1993. Other new artists winning first-place awards in the mid-1980s included Flora Roybal (*colcha*), Joseph T. Sanchez

(wood carving), and Joseph Blea (furniture). Between 1985 and 1989 the roster of prizewinning Spanish Market artists reflects the continually evolving skills of a number of artists who had appeared on the scene in the 1970s. Artists Anita Romero Jones, Marie Romero Cash, Ramón José López, Charles Carrillo, Monica Sosaya Halford, and Felix López dominated the market as first- and grand-prize winners, demonstrating their firm standing as contemporary leaders in the late-twentieth-century traditional Hispanic arts movement. Artists who received their first top or special honors during the late 1980s included Santana Salazar (weaving), Antonio Archuleta (furniture), Guadalupita Ortiz (retablos), Orlinda and Eurgencio López (wood carving), Michael Ortega (wood carving), Cordy Durán (weaving), Zoraida Ortega (weaving), Eulogio Ortega (bultos), Darlene Baros (*colcha*), Sabinita López Ortiz (wood carving), Juanita Jamarillo Lavadie (weaving), Alberto Delgado (tin), and Ellen Chávez de Leitner (retablos). **I**n 1990 the first Alan and Ann Vedder Memorial Award was presented to Maria Fernandez Graves of Ranchos de Taos for a *colcha* embroidery. The E. Boyd Memorial went to David Vigil of Albuquerque for his *reatas* (lariats) in

the newly added category of leather work. Santa Fean David Gonzales was awarded first place in the bulto category for a colonial-style carving, *Santo Niño Cautivo*. Tinsmith Jimmy Romero, son of Emilio and Senaida Romero, was honored with the Bienvenidos Award for the exceptional promise of his work. **S**anta Fe santero Frank Alarid, who took the 1990 top prize in the retablo category, was influenced by two

important advocates of his art: Santa Fe artist Randall Davey and E. Boyd. Alarid's father was working at Davey's Canyon Road estate when the ten-year-old caught the renowned painter's eye with his unpainted carvings. Davey taught Alarid the basics of painting and color, then introduced him to his neighbor, E. Boyd, who encouraged Alarid to take up the art of the traditional santero. Davey's death and a stint in the army resulted in a hiatus in Alarid's carving and painting career, but after a trip to the 1985 Spanish Market he began carving again with a new devotion. Alarid has exhibited at the Spanish Market every year

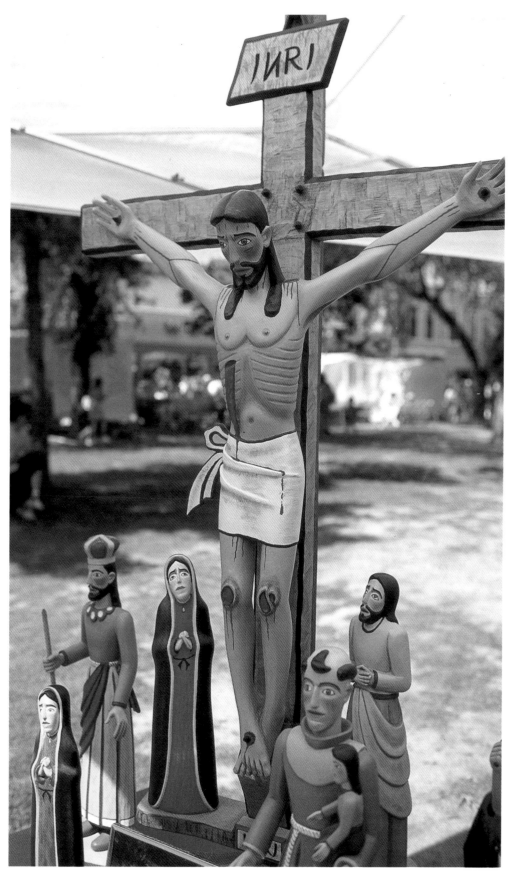

since 1987. The 1991 market brought new attention to the arts of straw appliqué and filigree jewelry with the prizewinning works of Jimmy Trujillo and Olivar Martínez. Trujillo, an Abiquiú native, became interested in the art of straw and cornhusk inlay in 1984. After intense research into the scant documentation about Spanish colonial methods and materials, Trujillo was soon creating a variety of innovative, traditionally styled straw and cornhusk crosses. He received first-place awards in 1991 and 1993 for his distinctive works in straw. Noted Española wood-carver Olivar Martínez expanded his artistry to encompass the uncommon art of filigree jewelry. His work was honored that year with the William Field Design Award, which is intended to encourage an artist of exceptional vision to advance his or her technical ability. Today Martínez is one of the few Spanish Market artists practicing the complex art. Other new artists to win first-place honors in 1991 were Jerry Sandoval (retablos), Karen Martínez (weaving), and Paul Martínez (furniture). Retired Santa Fe police officer Ernie Lujan took home the Hispanic Heritage Award for in-depth research in both 1991 and 1992. Donna Wright de Romero, daughter of Anita Romero Jones and a descendant of the distinguished Romero tinworker clan, made her Spanish Market debut by winning the Bienvenidos Award for her tinwork and *colcha* embroidery skills. In the Columbian Quincentenary year more artists participated in Spanish Market than ever before. Taos santero Gustavo Victor Goler earned both the grand prize and a first place in the bulto category that year. His rapid rise as one of the region's most celebrated santeros began in 1988, his first year in market, after many years of work conserving old santos. Goler's antique-looking bultos and retablos evoke the classical works of the eighteenth- and nineteenth-century master santeros. In 1990 he won the Hispanic Heritage Award for the in-depth research that is the foundation of all his work. The Alan and Ann Vedder Award was given to Goler in 1993, followed by the Spanish Market grand prize in 1994. Prizewinning tinsmiths Robert and Annie Romero and Fred Ray López are more recent masters. Robert Romero of Santa Fe, son and former student of master tinworkers Emilio and Senaida Romero, works with his wife, Annie. A tin chest by the couple earned them the 1991 first prize for tin, and their creative combination of tin and *colcha* embroidery in a traditional tin cross brought them top honors in the mixed-media category in 1992. The Romeros also received the 1994 Alan and Ann Vedder Award. Fred Ray López, a protégé of master tinsmith Angelina Delgado Martínez, was noted for his fresh approach to traditional motifs and design with first-place awards in tin in 1992, 1993, and 1994. Longtime santera Gloria López Córdova and her son Rafael López Córdova both took honors at the 1992 market. She received first prize in the mixed-media category, while a Córdova-style bulto by Rafael earned him the Alan and Ann Vedder Award. Finally, the 1992 introduction of utilitarian pottery and bone carving, two new, yet traditional art forms, demonstrates the ongoing process of discovery that contemporary Hispanic artists experience as they learn more about their artistic heritage. The 1993 awards

were dominated by a host of familiar names: Ramón José López, Lisa Trujillo, Charles Carrillo, Jimmy Trujillo, and Marie Romero Cash, but the talents of much newer artists were noted that year as well. Los Lunas santero Alcario Otero, a carpenter who entered the market just one year earlier, was recognized with a first prize in the bulto category. Lawrence Quintana, who first exhibited his furniture at market in 1989, took first place in that category for his intricately carved *Carreta para Gloria*. Veteran market weaver Karen Martínez was given the E. Boyd Memorial Award for originality and expressive design in her *Trampas Vallero* weaving. Other 1993 notables included Hispanic Heritage Award–winner James Córdova, a Santa Fe santero who made his Spanish Market debut in 1992. The art of straw appliqué was highlighted with the Bienvenidos Award given to straw artist Charlie Sánchez of Tomé and the Archbishop's Award given to Tim Valdez for a straw appliqué cross.

The distinguished career of Tesuque wood-carver Ben Ortega, who took the grand prize at the 1965 Spanish Market, came full circle at the 1994 market. Ortega's unpainted bulto *Moses and the Burning Bush* earned him first-place in the unpainted bulto category, confirming his lasting influence on that art form. Other veteran artists Felix López, winner in the painted bulto category, first-place weaver Lisa Trujillo, and Albuquerque santera Guadalupita Ortiz, who took first place in the mixed-media category, also showed their artistic stamina. Maria Fernandez Graves of Ranchos de Taos was cited for her fine *colcha* embroidery skills with a first place in that category, while santero Jerry Mondragón of Albuquerque took first prize in the retablo category.

The talents of emerging artists were applauded at the 1994 market as well. Santa Fe silversmith Lawrence Baca, a first-time market artist, took first place in the metals category for his elaborate silver monstrance. Baca's handmade silver crosses, rosaries, and other devotional objects echo the ecclesiastical themes of early Spanish colonial silversmiths and are highlighted by the artist's fine overlay and design skills. His prize-winning monstrance was purchased at the 1994 market by the society to add to its collection. Santa Fe furniture-maker and santero Raymond López, who entered market in 1993, took first prize in the furniture category for his hand-painted blanket chest in 1994. La Mesilla straw appliqué artist Krissa López, daughter of noted santero Felix López, made the leap from youth to adult exhibitor at the 1993 market. In 1994 she demonstrated her distinctive ability in straw among her adult peers, earning a first prize in the straw appliqué category. Finally, the intricate carving and painting skills exhibited by Santa Fe santero David Nabor Lucero in his painted bulto, *Arma Christi,* were recognized with the 1994 Hispanic Heritage Award for in-depth research. Another bulto by Lucero was also awarded the Archdiocese of Santa Fe's Archbishop's Award for its traditional portrayal of a religious theme. Seventy years after the first Spanish Market in 1926, the success of the Spanish Colonial Arts Society's annual summer and winter markets confirms that its goal to provide opportunities for artists to exhibit, sell, and grow in their work has been realized. As new talents

are tapped, Spanish Market gains influence and prestige as the country's premier exhibition of traditional Hispanic arts. This distinction is grounded in the creative power of the participating Spanish Market artists who have transformed the artistic expressions of the past into powerful symbols of a thriving contemporary culture.

FELIX LÓPEZ

In 1975, as a Spanish teacher at Española Valley High School, Felix López had no particular interest in Hispanic arts. He believed the key to preserving his culture was found between the covers of a Spanish textbook. But with the death of his father one year later, López was "reawakened" to his culture and to a new career in the arts. "When Dad died, we held a traditional *velorio* (wake) in the Penitente *morada* near our home in Santa Cruz," he says. "Dad was placed in front of the altar and surrounded by santos. The death was difficult, but the image was beautiful. It moved me so much, culturally, spiritually, that I knew I couldn't be my old self anymore." Feeling an urge to do something creative, López turned to his artistic younger brother, Alejandro, who taught him to make pottery. But working with clay was "too dirty" for his indoor studio, the family dining room, so López went out to the woodpile in hopes that carving would prove a cleaner craft. Carving tiny birds, bears, squirrels, and other animals at first, López suddenly saw crosses, torsos, and faces emerging from the wood. "The santos just started coming out of me," he recalls, "like magic."

Caught in the spell of traditional Hispanic art, López began visiting churches, museums, and *moradas* to learn more about santos. Using a pocketknife he concerned himself first with the shape of the wood, leaving his bultos unpainted in order to concentrate on perfecting body and facial features. But the santos looked unfinished to López, and he later applied acrylics to his pieces. Later still, he returned to the painting techniques of some of the early santeros, developing the rich, subtle colors of his predecessors through the use of all-natural pigments. Meanwhile, López experimented in another traditional art form: straw appliqué. He worked in that medium for about seven years, creating straw crosses and chests, and then decided to devote all of his energy to carving. "For a long time, I was so high from the

103. *St. Francis of Assisi, 1992.*

morada experience that I wanted to do everything," he says. "But I decided I needed to focus if I wanted to be the best I could." Today López continues to push himself to his full potential. His innovative interpretations of traditional bultos combine the range of his skills and experience. For example, he might incorporate straw into his work for added detail or take liberty with traditional iconography, such as slitting openings in the rays that flank an image of Our Lady of Guadalupe. "There's a lot of room for creativity in doing traditional work," López says. "You can do different things that haven't been done before and it's still a traditional piece." López's Spanish Market involvement began in 1977 and follows much the same course as his career. During his early years in the market he exhibited unpainted santos and straw appliqué; today he displays colorful, sophisticated depictions of the saints. He has been recognized with a number of Spanish Market awards in both categories, including the 1994 first prize for bultos.

Two pieces by López included in the society's collection reflect his artistic evolution. His simple straw appliqué cross was made in 1977. A finely detailed Saint Francis bulto with cross in hand and a skull at his feet was created in 1992. After retiring from his teaching job in 1991, López now lives in La Mesilla and works full-time as an artist. In 1987 he was one of thirty artists in the country selected to participate in "Hispanic Art in the United States," a traveling exhibition organized by the Museum of Fine Arts in Houston, Texas. His works have also been exhibited at the Smithsonian Institution, the Heard Museum, and the Albuquerque Museum. Despite his recognition, do not expect to find López at some international exhibit during the month of July. "Every July, you'll find me in a Spanish Market booth in Santa Fe," he says. "The market inspires me to create, and it reminds me that I should never let myself get too far away from home."

RAMÓN JOSÉ LÓPEZ

Throughout his childhood in Santa Fe Ramón José López was keenly aware of the religious mystique surrounding the "City of the Holy Faith." "The santos, the holy processions, the incredible faith of the people," López recalls. "I knew I was lucky to have been born in such a special place, and it was like it was in my blood to express my feelings about it. But I had no idea why or how." In a search for the answers López turned to art. As a teenager he learned to work metal with the hope that it would lead him to a career as a sculptor. Then in 1974, after marrying his wife, Nance, a jeweler, he abandoned sculpting and concentrated on making jewelry. Although he was skilled in both, neither medium truly pacified López's creative restlessness. In 1981 he discovered something that did: Spanish colonial art. "I realized how beautiful the old things were, how much history there was in these works of art," López says. "I knew I had found a way to express the depth of my culture." Drawing on his metalworking skills López first experimented with traditional hand-raising methods, using thousands of hand-hammered blows to shape silver into hollowware bowls, candlestick holders, and chalices. His skills as a silversmith gained him entry to his first Spanish Market in 1981, at which time he began an intense study of Spanish colonial metalwork. It was while studying public and private collections that López was seduced by the vibrant color and intense emotion of eighteenth- and nineteenth-century retablos and bultos. The works of santeros such as José Rafael Aragón moved him spiritually and artistically in a way he had never known before. López knew he had found the calling that had eluded him for years. Before long he discovered why: Nearly thirty years before López was born, his grandfather, Don Lorenzo López, had been a well-known Santa Fe wood-carver. "My family never talked about my grandfather's art, so I never even knew that the tradition was in my family," he says. "Once I learned about it, everything just came together." Embracing his grandfather's creative spirit, López took his grandfather's adz and began carving figures the way Don Lorenzo once had, using native pine,

104. *Crucifixion* in mica-glazed silver frame, 1988. 105. *Holy Family*, 1994, painting on hide.

105

aspen, and cottonwood. Known for his hand-carved burros and *carretas* (carts) with oxen, López's grandfather rarely made santos. Unlike his grandfather, however, the younger López concentrated on carving and painting religious bultos and retablos. Immersing himself in research on traditional iconography and techniques, López experimented with natural pigments until he achieved the warm, vibrant colors for which his work is now noted. Next he combined his fine metalworking skills with his detailed images, embellishing the objects with silver and other materials to give them a more contemporary feel. His distinctive retablos, for example, are framed in silver, then overlaid with mica, giving them a glossy, graceful depth. "My work is traditional, but I'm a contemporary artist," he says. "I'm taking religious images that have been produced in New Mexico throughout history and stepping them up a little." In addition to silverwork, López began exhibiting bultos, retablos, *reredos, escudos* (small silver-framed religious images), and furniture at Spanish Market in 1985, where his unique style has since brought him numerous awards. His work also has been exhibited and included in collections nationwide, among them the Smithsonian Institution, the Heard Museum, the Museum of International Folk Art, and the Taylor Museum of the Colorado Springs Fine Arts Center. Five of López's works—two *escudos,* a hollowware serving dish, a decorative silver drum, and a hide painting—are included in the society's collection and demonstrate the range of López's skill. Two of his grandfather's trademark *carretas* with oxen are also in the collection. López's four children, who are learning Spanish colonial methods from their father, are also regular Spanish Market participants. "The Spanish Market has given me lots of opportunities and exposure," he says. "Now, it's also giving my children the chance to continue the tradition that my grandfather, their great-grandfather, began in Santa Fe so long ago."

106. Tin frame, 1975.

As a little girl growing up in Santa Fe, Angelina Delgado Martínez believed her grandparents lived in a house made of tin. "People would come from the East, from all over, and ask if this was the house of tin," she recalls. "For a while I thought they meant that the house was made of tin. I didn't understand what they meant. I was very young and had no desire to be an artist. I wanted to be a ballerina." Although their Canyon Road home was made of adobe, it was filled with tin. Home to Delgado Martínez's grandfather, acclaimed New Mexico tinsmith Francisco Delgado, the house also served as a shop from which Delgado sold his elaborate works in tin. It was the same house in which her father, Ildeberto (Eddie) Delgado, had been trained by his father as a tinsmith. And it was the place where she, too, would develop her talents—not as a ballerina but as a traditional maker of tin. A frequent visitor to her grandfather's house, young Angelina was enamored by the shiny "poor man's silver" that he and her father fashioned into decorative and utilitarian objects. Before long she was creating miniature replicas of their work alongside them. At twelve, she sold in her grandfather's shop her first chandelier, a four-inch version with birthday candle lights for five dollars. By the time she reached high school she was doing custom work, integrating the traditional patterns made by her grandfather and father into her own graceful style. "I took the tools and the skills my grandfather and father had passed on to me and decided to devote myself to preserving this craft that is so much a part of our culture," she says. "As a third-generation Delgado, I knew that tin would always be an

important part of my life." After her grandfather and father died, Delgado Martínez became the sole representative of her family tradition. A teacher by profession, she spent her spare time creating tin frames, *nichos,* sconces, candlesticks, chandeliers, and other traditional items. She often combined the tin with glass, wallpaper, or *colcha* embroidery for added decoration. Entering her first Spanish Market in 1968, Delgado Martínez was one of the first tinsmiths to exhibit there. She has participated in the market almost every year since, winning numerous first-place awards in the tin category and the 1991 Master's Award for Lifetime Achievement. "The Spanish Market has given me many opportunities as an artist," she says. Delgado Martínez has now clipped, crimped, stamped, scored, and soldered for nearly sixty years, forging a name for herself as one of the only female tinsmiths of her generation. Her daughter, Rita Younis, who recently learned the art from her mother, now also represents the family tradition at Spanish Market. A prime example of Delgado Martínez's talents, a tin mirror, is included in the society's collection. Described by the artist as a "Francisco Classic," the design is based on one her grandfather used and features hand-scored columns and diagonal corner pieces surrounded by repeated hand-stamped motifs. In 1984 Delgado Martínez received the New Mexico Governor's Award for Excellence in the Arts. Her work is featured in collections at the Taylor Museum of the Colorado Springs Fine Arts Center, the Museum of International Folk Art, the Albuquerque Museum, and the Museo Archaeológico in Madrid, Spain.

ELISEO AND PAULA RODRÍGUEZ

A fire is crackling in a corner of the cozy Santa Fe adobe home of Eliseo and Paula Rodríguez, and it breathes the sweet smell of piñon into the small dining room that doubles as the couple's work studio. Here beside a long table strewn with razor blades, wheat straw, and sugar pine wood, they sit quietly, pensively, as each gently applies single pieces of straw to black matte crosses that have been shaped from the wood. **P**aula Rodríguez creates intricate floral patterns that burst forth from a small cross in a flurry of gold, while her husband re-creates the lives of the saints in a complex series of tableaux on an astounding eight-foot-tall cross. With each piece of straw, the couple brings new dimensions to the projects at hand—and to the ancient art of straw appliqué.

107. Eliseo Rodríguez, *Stations of the Cross*, 1982. Bequest of Alan and Ann Vedder.

Had it not been for Eliseo and Paula Rodríguez, the straw appliqué technique today might have been relegated to the annals of New Mexico history. In 1936, after spending many years developing his skills as a painter and woodworker, Santa Fe native Eliseo inspired the rebirth of the age-old art. Attracted to the complex straw objects he had seen in museums and area homes, Eliseo gladly accepted his New Mexico Federal Art Project task of reviving the ancient straw appliqué process. Newly married at the time, Paula, who grew up in Rowe, soon joined her husband in his research and experimentation. The painstaking but beautiful art became the couple's creative passion. "**I** was interested in reviving something that had not been done in a long, long time," Eliseo recalls. "It was a very exciting time." Adds Paula: "But it wasn't easy. There were no examples to look at, nobody to teach how to do it. Eliseo became the teacher and I watched and learned from him. We just did what we could." **D**uring the next three decades the couple refined their materials and techniques and soon established themselves as true masters of their craft. Although extant works in straw were usually geometric and occasionally floral in design, Eliseo and Paula

integrated narrative themes, such as the stations of the cross and nativity scenes, into traditional crosses, boxes, and chests. Successfully depicting biblical stories in the medium was a major feat. Today they are perhaps best known for their extraordinary mosaics in straw. **I**n the 1970s the couple took their talents to Spanish Market. "We were a few of the only ones to do straw at the market for a very long time," says Paula. "But after a while, others began to get into it. That made us happy to see that the tradition was being passed on." **T**he exquisite artistry of the Rodríguezes' work influenced succeeding generations of artists, including their daughters Vicki Rodríguez and Yolanda Griego, both accomplished straw artists and regular Spanish Market exhibitors.

Of their eleven grandchildren, four also have taken up the art, learning the process from their grandparents at the couple's busy dining room table. The grandchildren are also regular Spanish Market participants. **T**he couple's work has been recognized worldwide and is included in collections at the Museum of International Folk Art, the Smithsonian Institution, the Millicent Rogers Museum, and the Albuquerque Museum, as well as in private collections in Germany, England, and Mexico. They have been honored as recipients of the New Mexico Governor's Award for Excellence in the Arts and through the years have garnered countless Spanish Market awards. Two straw crosses included in the society's collection are examples of the Rodríguezes' extraordinary work. "**I**n this day and age, things seem to be passing by like a shadow," says Eliseo. "But the Spanish Market encourages young artists to pursue their work. It has been a great thing for us and is a great thing for those who take advantage of it."

108. Paula Rodríguez, *St. Francis of Assisi*, 1986.

Every day by early morning Emilio and Senaida Romero are seated at the long rectangular table that dominates their Santa Fe kitchen. Assorted shiny scraps of tin are scattered on the tabletop, and the couple is busy clipping, hammering, and stamping them into a variety of shapes. Meanwhile, the phone rings, a pot on the stove boils, children and grandchildren stop by to chat. Unfazed, they answer the phone calls, tend to the cooking, and visit with the family—without missing a punch, snip, or snap. **I**t's all in a day's work for these renowned master tinsmiths, who for more than forty years have been crafting some of the finest examples of Spanish colonial tinwork anywhere. While some artists prefer the quiet solitude of a private studio, the Romeros thrive on the frenetic energy that surrounds their home and work space. From the kitchen table where their religious, decorative, and utilitarian objects are created to the generations of children and grandchildren they have inspired to pursue careers in the arts, the Romeros have made their art a way of life. "**T**here's always something creative going on in our house, and that's how we like it," Emilio says. Adds Senaida: "Our family was born punching, and we're going to die punching." **M**arried for nearly seventy years, the Romeros grew up surrounded by the tin tradition. Senaida is a native of Glorieta, where her grandfather was a well-known tinsmith. Emilio, who was reared in Santa Fe, recalls collecting empty lard and kerosene cans as a youth to sell to area tinsmiths. About 1937 he was trained as a professional sheet-metal worker in the camps of the Civilian Conservation Corps. He worked in the field throughout World War II, after which time he and Senaida began to explore the artistic possibilities of tin. "**T**he greatest challenge of working tin was the layout, but being a metalworker, I could lay out most anything," Emilio recalls. "We always loved the old-time tinwork and we started duplicating those pieces. Then we just tried to be creative." **T**he Romeros' experimentation and collaborative techniques produced some of the most inno-

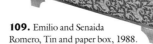

109. Emilio and Senaida Romero, Tin and paper box, 1988.

110. Emilio Romero, Tin frame with wool textile by Ortega Weavers, Chimayó, 1974.

vative tinwork to date. Their wide-ranging work includes church and devotional items—tin crosses and *nichos* designed to hold saints, as well as functional objects such as mirrors, picture frames, chandeliers, and candlestick holders. Adapting to the times, the couple added wastebaskets and light-switch plates to their repertoire. Senaida, a skilled *colcha* embroiderer, combined *colcha* and other textiles with tin to create new and unique wall decorations. **I**n the late 1960s the Romeros began exhibiting their work at Spanish Market. "The market was one of the best things to happen to the people of Santa Fe," says Senaida. "It gives artists a say-so, a voice." Known for selling out their collection at the market by noon, the couple has earned numerous awards and in 1988 became the society's first recipients of the Master's Award for Lifetime Achievement. Two of their works, a traditional "double eagle" sconce and a mirror with textile borders, are included in the society's collection. **T**he Romeros' artistry has been recognized worldwide and is included in collections at the Smithsonian Institution, as well as in Australia and Latin America. In 1987 the couple became the first team to receive a prestigious National Heritage Fellowship for artistic excellence from the National Endowment for the Arts. In a catalogue about the National Heritage Fellows, a writer described the precision of the couple's teamwork as "hard to tell where one ends and the other begins." **P**erhaps the Romeros' most notable achievement has been their influence on the artistic pursuits of their seven children and numerous grandchildren. Of their progeny, Marie Romero Cash, Anita Romero Jones, Jimmie Romero, Robert Romero, and Donna Romero Wright are regular Spanish Market participants. With skills ranging from tinwork, painting, and carving to *colcha* embroidery and straw appliqué, the Romero family is acclaimed as one of New Mexico's first families of Spanish colonial art. "**I** don't want to brag about it, but I have to tell the truth," Emilio says with a grin. "My kids are very talented. They're really great artists."

LUIS TAPIA

During the late 1960s a storm of social consciousness brewed among young Hispanics in Santa Fe, and a call for cultural unity, *"Viva la Raza,"* rang through city streets. Luis Tapia, then a restless teenager, heeded the call. "The activism of the sixties motivated me to educate myself, to learn what my culture was really about," recalls Tapia. "I began realizing that we had our own art, our own music. I had been living that all of my life but was never really aware of it. I decided to become aware." With encouragement from his former wife, Star, Tapia began his cultural education among the collections of seventeenth- through nineteenth-century Spanish colonial art at the Museum of International Folk Art. The profound historic and spiritual value of the utilitarian and religious objects Tapia saw there inspired him. Carving small-scale nude sculptures at first, he soon began making and restoring santos with the careful purpose of preserving the artistic techniques, motifs, and materials that his forebears had developed. A few years later he began to build and restore colonial furniture as well. In the early 1970s Tapia entered his first Spanish Market, where his diligence and talent did not go unnoticed. In 1975 Tapia won first prize in the wood-carving category for his traditional painted bultos. The first artist ever to exhibit furniture at the market, Tapia also took first and second prizes in that medium that year. "The Spanish Market was my first step as an artist in the public eye," says Tapia. "As with any new artist who goes into the market, it gave me a good foundation for understanding what the culture's about and what people are doing." At the time, Tapia recalls, Spanish Market was still a small gathering of no more than thirty artists. Few of them painted santos, opting instead to stress the natural wood grain. The use of color, however, was a main ingredient in Tapia's work, and he continually experimented with natural pigments and homemade gesso to achieve as brilliant colors as possible. Not satisfied with the muted hues the natural pigments produced, he turned to watercolors and egg tempera, then finally to commercial gesso and acrylics. It was a step that was considered a bold departure from traditional methods but one that established Tapia's unique sense of artistry and style.

111. *St. Michael and the Dragon, 1975.*

112. *St. Dismas, 1993.*

"I liked the brightness, the clarity, and the workability of acrylics a lot," he says. "I just moved on to a more vibrant palette of color, but I maintained a primitive carving style." In time Tapia began to take risks with traditional imagery, breaking away from the established iconography in ways never seen before. Whether changing a simple gesture or the entire context in which saints or other religious images were traditionally portrayed, Tapia's interpretation proved individualistic—and controversial.

"I took traditional themes and blended them with my own ideas about contemporary life," he says. "Some people saw that as me abandoning my tradition, but I saw it as putting new life into the tradition." Tapia's more modernist vision continued to grow, and in 1978 he left Spanish Market to pursue a career as a contemporary artist. In no time his works were being exhibited and collected by museums and individuals nationwide, including the Smithsonian Institution, the Museum of American Folk Art, the Heard Museum, the Museum of International Folk Art, and the Gene Autry Western Heritage Museum. Today his work is represented exclusively by Owings-Dewey Fine Art Gallery in Santa Fe.

The evolution of Tapia's artistry, from his entrance into Spanish Market in the early 1970s to today, is clearly illustrated by two pieces of his work that are included in the society's collection. The first piece, a 1975 cottonwood bulto of Saint Michael, duplicates the traditional iconography of the saint in terms of Tapia's use of imagery and form, although his application of egg tempera gives the piece a bright, polished exterior rather than an antique look. The second piece, Tapia's 1993 pine *Saint Dismas* crucifix, on the other hand, is experimental in style and theme. Known as the patron saint of prisoners, Saint Dismas was crucified alongside Christ. Using pine and acrylics Tapia portrays the saint as a *pinto,* or prisoner, with tattoos drawn on his hands, legs, and chest—including one that bears his prison identification number.

"I strive to be fresh with my work all of the time so that I can continue to develop my own style," Tapia says. "But to this day I still send young artists to the Spanish Market. It's a good place for an artist to get a start."

In 1984 Irvin Trujillo was taken with technology. Having just earned a degree in civil engineering from the University of New Mexico, he was geared for a high-tech career in a city miles away from the pastoral Chimayó farm where he was raised. His philosophy: "If a machine can do it better and faster than a human, then why should a human do it?" But Trujillo's true sensibilities were far from his technical training. A seventh-generation weaver whose family had practiced their art and farmed for centuries in Chimayó, Trujillo always dreamed of one day returning to the family's Centinela Ranch to weave full-time. In fact, as early as 1977, he had been exhibiting his weavings at Spanish Market. But times were much different from when his ancestors balanced farming with weaving. He had an education and financial opportunities his ancestors never had. "It seemed silly to give all that up," he recalls. But after a short stint with the U.S. Corps of Engineers, Trujillo realized his heart was on the farm. Together with his new wife, Lisa, herself a beginning weaver at the time, Trujillo looked to the future with a dream of establishing a weaving cooperative at the ranch someday. "Our goal was to maintain the family tradition," Trujillo says, "but also to be able to keep up with the changing times." The couple returned to Chimayó in 1984 and never looked back. Two years later the Trujillos began constructing their dream as they added a studio and gallery to the existing weaving business. The mission behind their new business, Centinela Traditional Arts, was to allow visitors to witness the weaving process as well as to purchase traditional Rio Grande style weavings made by the Trujillos and other area weavers. Situated in a modest tin-roofed adobe on the ancient family ranch, the weaving studio today serves as an exhibition space for at least fifteen weavers. A small exhibit honoring Trujillo's late father, Jacobo, a renowned master of the Chimayó weaving style, gives visitors a glimpse of the important role the Trujillo family has played in the Chimayó weaving industry for generations. "My father always told me to grasp onto my roots—the weaving— because nobody could ever take that knowledge away," he says. Jacobo Trujillo began passing that knowledge on to his son when Irvin was ten. Standing alongside his father at the elder Trujillo's massive wooden loom, Irvin learned the intricate stitches that characterize the Chimayó weaving style, which he describes as "a combination of the Saltillo, Vallero, and Rio Grande styles that evolved from Mexican, Anglo, and Pueblo and Navajo Indian influences." Following his father's philosophy of designing one-of-a-kind pieces, he also learned to value quality over quantity. Says Irvin: "My father believed that if

you made each weaving unique, you would learn something important from each one." Taking his father's traditional instruction, Irvin used his own technical training to begin to explore more contemporary motifs. The resulting weavings were complex in design and highlighted by bright colors and extreme contrasts. "I try to capture the spirit of the old pieces while also expressing my own experience in the contemporary world," he says. An untitled weaving by Trujillo in the society's collection exemplifies his meticulous application of traditional techniques and his exquisite sense of design and color. Other pieces by Trujillo have been included in exhibits and collections nationwide, including at the Smithsonian Institution and the Heard Museum. Before his death in 1990, Jacobo Trujillo encouraged Irvin's wife, Lisa, in her weaving pursuits and praised her natural affinity for the art.

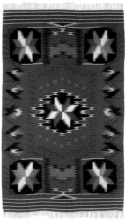

113. Irvin Trujillo, *Untitled Vallero*, 1992.

"(Lisa's) not only a weaver, she's an artist, one of the best," the elder Trujillo said in an interview for the 1990 *Spanish Market Magazine*. Lisa began weaving shortly after her marriage to Irvin in 1982, and although not Hispanic she has made the tradition her own. In time she was weaving her own exceptional textiles—bold, geometric variations on the Rio Grande style—as well as hand-spinning and dyeing wool with natural pigments. "I try to stick close to the tradition," Lisa says. "My influence obviously comes from Irvin and Jake [Jacobo], but my approach is different than theirs. My work, my style, my designs are definitely my own." In addition to exhibiting their works at their Chimayó gallery and studio, the Trujillos are regular exhibitors at the Spanish Market. In 1991 Irvin Trujillo received the coveted Best of Show Award for his weaving, *La Entriega*. And as a testament to the strength of the family weaving tradition, he was awarded the annual Jake O. Trujillo Award for Excellence in Weaving at the 1992 Spanish Market. Lisa, meanwhile, won the award in 1993 and 1994. "The Spanish Market, like weaving, has been a tradition in my family," Irvin says. Adds Lisa: "It's been valuable exposure for both of us."

HORACIO VALDEZ

When Horacio Valdez died on August 16, 1992, he had just returned from Sunday Mass and retired to his bedroom for a midday nap. Shortly after a visitor appeared: Doña Sebastiana had come to carry the sixty-three-year-old santero away in her rickety cart of death. Like the man himself, it was a quiet ending to a quiet life. **V**aldez's unassuming ending, like his artistic career, had a resounding impact on his fellow artists, friends, and peers. A man widely considered to be a modern-day master of santero art, he is credited with inspiring a return to the polychromed images of the eighteenth and nineteenth centuries from the unpainted carving style made popular by the Córdova wood-carvers in the early twentieth century. His bold acrylic surfaces vibrate with the life of the saints he depicted in his refined repertoire of bultos, and his distinctive *carretas de la muerte* (death carts) display his precision carving skills. "**H**e was the santeros' santero," says Santa Fe santero Charles Carrillo. Adds Luis Tapia: "The work of Horacio Valdez is an inspiration to us all." **B**orn in the tiny northern New Mexico community of Dixon, Valdez later moved just up the hill to where the village of Apodaca overlooks a narrow valley. By the age of forty-five he had spent some twenty-five years working as a professional carpenter in the area, but a 1974 accident resulted in an injury that confined him to home. **A** devout Catholic and a member of the Penitente Brotherhood, Valdez found comfort in the faces of the ancient santos he saw in the local church and *morada*. To pass the time he picked up a pocketknife and began carving copies of the santos from random chunks of wood he found scattered around his home. Soon his simple pastime had become a serious passion, one that would forever change Valdez's life. "**W**hen I first started, I didn't really know what I was doing, so I sent for some books on santos from the Taylor Museum in Colorado Springs," Valdez recalled in a July 1986 *New Mexico Magazine* interview with Española writer Jim Sagel. In a July 24–30, 1992, *Pasatiempo* interview one month before his death he added, "I started carving and the pieces started selling, and before long, I had just changed jobs from a carpenter to a santero. It was just a blessing from God." **A** self-taught carver, Valdez was also a self-taught painter. Unsure of what paints to use, Valdez went to a store where a clerk suggested he try acrylics. Though his use of commercial paints was a significant departure from the works of the early santeros, who mostly used paints derived from natural pigments, Valdez's work was bright, bold, and refreshingly new. Recalls

114. Death cart, 1992.

Luis Tapia, whose own unique creations are distinguished by their brilliant color: "Horacio's work immediately made a statement that this work was not just traditional; it was also very new." Along with his glowing colors and refined symmetry of form, Valdez's deep spirituality also comes through in his works. From the best-known to the least celebrated of saints, his detailed pieces underscore the mystery and folklore behind the legendary images. With large, pensive eyes sitting beneath sorrowful brows, Valdez's santos tell tales of compassion, persecution, and above all, faith. Although his eerie *carretas de la muerte* were a favorite among collectors of his works, his personal favorite was the crucifix, the symbol of the Brotherhood of Jesus Christ. Valdez created more than two hundred crucifixes throughout his career, including one that was presented to Pope John Paul II in 1979. Another, a masterpiece crucifix six and a half feet tall, was a donation from Valdez to his local parish, St. Anthony's Church in Dixon. The Holy Family Church in Chimayó is also home to the artist's fourteen-piece *Stations of the Cross,* another of the artist's greatest works. Valdez entered Spanish Market in the early 1970s. For more than a decade his work was honored with numerous market awards, including the 1984 Norma Fiske Day Award, which honors one of the society's earliest supporters. Although he quit exhibiting at Spanish Market soon after, Valdez returned to the market one last time before his death in 1992, when his achievements were honored with a special exhibition of his work. One of Valdez's extraordinary death carts is also included in the society's collection. In the nearly twenty years encompassing Valdez's carving career, his work was acquired by the Gene Autry Western Heritage Museum, the Smithsonian Institution, the Millicent Rogers Museum, the Museum of International Folk Art, and the Albuquerque Museum. Valdez, unpretentious to the end, was never much for awards or exhibits; he would rather have sold his works from home than deal with galleries or museums. Working alone in his isolated Apodaca workshop, Valdez relished the quiet life. It was a life where God was never too far away from a simple man and his treasured pocketknife. "It seems like I get closer to God when I'm carving," he said in the 1992 interview. "I pray a little bit and think good thoughts, and pray a little more that the carving will come out right. I find joy in working because I realize that I am working with God and God is working with me."

115. Rhonda Crespín Bertholf, *The Visitation*, 1994.
116. Raymond López, *Our Lady of Sorrows/Dolores*, 1994. Gift of artist.
117. Victor Goler, *St. Veronica*, 1992.
118. Frank Alarid, *St. Gabriel*, 1995.
119. Frank Brito, *Nativity*, 1994.

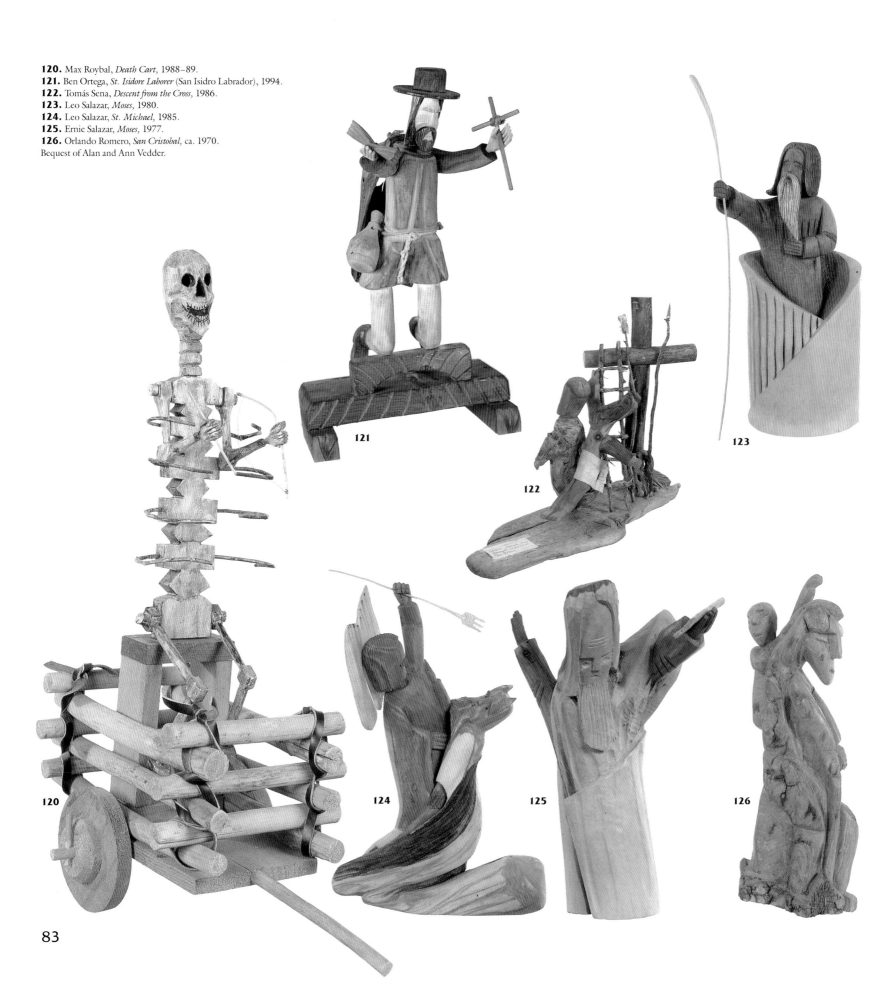

120. Max Roybal, *Death Cart,* 1988–89.
121. Ben Ortega, *St. Isidore Laborer* (San Isidro Labrador), 1994.
122. Tomás Sena, *Descent from the Cross,* 1986.
123. Leo Salazar, *Moses,* 1980.
124. Leo Salazar, *St. Michael,* 1985.
125. Ernie Salazar, *Moses,* 1977.
126. Orlando Romero, *San Cristobal,* ca. 1970.
Bequest of Alan and Ann Vedder.

121

123

122

120

124

125

126

83

127. Marco Oviedo, Noisemaker (*Matraca*), 1985.
128. Sammy Córdova, *St. Francis*, 1981.
129. Mariano A. Chávez, *Manger with Donkeys*, 1975.
130. Camilla Trujillo, Micaceous pot, 1993.
131. David Nabor Lucero,
St. Anne with the Virgin Mary as a Child, 1995.

127

130

128

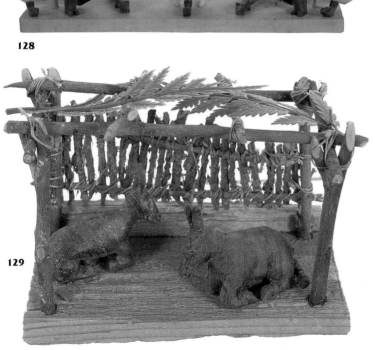

129

131

132

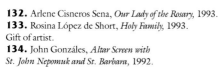

132. Arlene Cisneros Sena, *Our Lady of the Rosary,* 1993.
133. Rosina López de Short, *Holy Family,* 1993.
Gift of artist.
134. John Gonzáles, *Altar Screen with
St. John Nepomuk and St. Barbara,* 1992.

133

134

135. Star Tapia, Rawhide box, 1977.
136. Vicki Rodríguez, Straw appliqué box, 1986.
137. William Cabrera, Chest, 1988.
138. Jimmy Romero, Tin and paper box, 1990.
139. Lawrence Baca, Silver monstrance, 1994.
140. Olivar Martínez, Silver filigree
necklace and earrings, 1991.
141. Monica Sosaya Halford, *Colcha* embroidered altar screen, 1991.
142. Robert Romero, Tin double-headed eagle reliquary, 1995.

142

143   144   145

143. Maria Luisa Delgado Roybal, Tin *nicho,* 1978.
144. Tomás Arrey, Hand-forged iron crucifix, 1994.
145. Rolando de Leon, Hand-forged iron spoon, 1977.
146. María Vergara Wilson, *Techos de Trampas,* 1991, ikat blanket.
147. María Vergara Wilson, Ikat blanket, 1979.
148. María Elena Leitner, Rio Grande blanket, 1994.
149. Karen Martínez, Saltillo Rio Grande blanket, 1995.

146

148

147

149

150

151

152

150. Timothy Valdez, Straw appliqué cross, 1990. Gift of artist.

151. Mrs. Thomas Benrimo, Straw appliqué cross, 1968. Bequest of Rebecca Salsbury James.

152. Felix López, Straw appliqué cross, 1977.

153. Vicki Rodríquez, Straw appliqué cross, 1985.

154. Jimmy Trujillo, *Por Nuestro Pecado (For Our Sins)*, 1993, straw appliqué cross.

155. Felix López, Straw appliqué cross, 1985. Bequest of Alan and Ann Vedder.

153

154

155

Daybed, 19th century,
Spanish Colonial Arts Society Collection
on loan to El Rancho de las Golondrinas Museum.

Appendix A: The Spanish Colonial Arts Society Collection: A History

DONNA PIERCE

The Spanish Colonial Arts Society collection presently contains some 2,500 pieces; all but 35 were secured after 1951. The first items were collected by Frank G. Applegate before 1929; the latest additions come from society purchases made at the annual Spanish Market. Some sixty-six years, first of sporadic and then of sustained work, have produced a unique collection of New Mexican traditional art and material culture that focuses not only on religious art and furniture but also on the implements of daily life from the colonial period and the nineteenth century. The collection includes household utensils, agricultural tools, livestock equipment, weapons, horse gear, personal clothing, jewelry, accessories, and other miscellaneous items. Prior to incorporation in 1929, the Spanish Colonial Arts Society had acquired examples of New Mexican traditional arts, primarily religious, in order to prevent them from being taken from the state. Under the direction of Applegate, who had been collecting such works personally since the early 1920s, the society started to assemble what Mary Austin called "a permanent collection of the best examples of the old work, and, as we had the means, to collect them and place them on exhibition in the rooms of the Historical Society in the Old Palace (of the Governors Museum)."[1] The first object listed in the acquisition records is an altar screen by José Rafael Aragón from the church of Llano Quemado.[2] The old altar screen had been removed from the church and replaced by a new one made by the village carpenter, who incorporated milled moldings. Frank Applegate was contacted in 1928 and went to Llano Quemado, where he met with church committee members. At that time he purchased the old altar screen for five hundred dollars, but determined that the altar table upon which it had rested was too rotten to salvage. In 1929 the altar screen was installed in the Palace of the Governors, where it remains on view today. The society's second major acquisition, the famous private chapel, the Santuario at Chimayó, was immediately deeded to the Archdiocese of Santa Fe. Efforts were also made to acquire some of the Santuario objects that already had been sold, among them the small statue of Santiago (Saint James), a bulto that was eventually repurchased and returned to the main altar of the chapel. Other pieces were either returned to the chapel or deposited in the society's or in other museum collections within the state. During the next few years following incorporation, the Spanish Colonial Arts Society continued to purchase objects and receive donations for the collection under the guidance of Applegate, who had been appointed its first curator. The board of trustees formed the Committee on a Permanent Collection, with Santa Fe artist Andrew Dasburg as chair and philanthropist Mary Cabot Wheelwright, Santa Fe artist Gustave Baumann, and Albuquerquean Herman Schweizer, head of the Fred Harvey Company Indian Department, as members. In these early years Wheelwright frequently donated objects to the society's collection.[3] A committee composed of Dr. Frank E. Mera, architect John Gaw Meem, and Frank Applegate served as liaison to the Historical Society of New Mexico, which operated the exhibitions in the Palace of the Governors. With Frank Applegate's untimely death in February 1931, the society made its next major acquisition: items from Applegate's personal collection of Spanish traditional arts. Mary Austin chaired a committee to raise funds to purchase twenty bultos, fifteen retablos, and one piece of *colcha* embroidery from Applegate's widow Alta. Austin tried to place other pieces from Applegate's collection with private New Mexico collectors, presumably to prevent their acquisition by dealers and subsequent sale outside the state. During this period, objects collected by the society were loaned to the Palace of the Governors for exhibition. The Spanish Colonial Arts Society appears to have been largely dormant from August 1934, when Mary Austin died, until 1938, when Leonora F. Curtin led a short-lived reactivation. After the Taylor Museum in Colorado Springs purchased religious folk art from Arroyo Hondo, Santa Fe district public health officer Dr. Harry P. Mera exhorted the society to resume efforts to acquire objects for its collection and was nominated as chairperson of the new Collections Committee. Nina Otero-Warren proposed the formation of a committee to "ask the clergy to prevent the sale of Santos from the Churches." Exhibition needs were discussed but not until summer 1938 was a new agreement negotiated with Edgar Lee

156. E. Boyd cleaning a retablo, ca. 1958.

Hewett of the Museum of New Mexico for a special exhibition devoted exclusively to Spanish colonial arts at the Palace of the Governors. According to the loan agreement, the society had forty-eight items on exhibition at the Palace, including hide paintings, Rio Grande blankets, *colcha* embroideries, Mexican *rebozos,* altar cloths, bultos, and retablos.[4] There seem to have been no additions to the collection throughout the 1940s, when society activity was suspended. Ina Sizer Cassidy attempted to revive the society again in 1949, but her efforts proved unsuccessful until 1951, when E. Boyd joined her and served as a catalyst to revitalize the organization in an enduring way. During early reorganization meetings in the spring of 1952 a Collections Committee was formed to approve purchases and receive donations to the permanent collection. Indeed, objects donated to the collection

were processed as early as 1952, with board members making numerous gifts during this early period.[5] In a 1954 leaflet soliciting memberships in the revived Spanish Colonial Arts Society, E. Boyd reiterated the society's desire to retain objects in-state:

157. Leonora Curtin Paloheimo, ca. 1975.

A small group of the original members, together with other interested persons, felt that there was a real need for an active and energetic group to promote the aims set out by the original Society, to collect more material and to arrange for the safekeeping and display of the material already in the Society's collection. . . . By the purchase of unique examples which might otherwise have been removed from this region, or simply destroyed in the path of progress, the Society has saved, and is now saving, many rare items which can never be duplicated.

During the 1940s the permanent collection of the Spanish Colonial Arts Society remained at the Palace museum under the care of Curator of Archaeology Marjorie Lambert.[6] To protect the identity of the collection while the society was inactive, Lambert catalogued the objects into the collection of the Historical Society of New Mexico, a long-associated organization with an overlapping membership. Then, in 1952 Lambert assisted Boyd in identifying the society's objects and recataloguing them into its own collection. Upon completion of the Museum of International Folk Art of the Museum of New Mexico in 1953, the Spanish Colonial Arts Society collection was moved from the Palace of the Governors to this new location, where most of it con-

tinues to be housed. In May 1954 E. Boyd published a *Hand List of the Collection of the Spanish Colonial Arts Society, Inc.,* describing the 140 items in the collection at that time. Thirty-five objects were identified as from the original collection; the remainder had been acquired in the brief two-year period since reactivation. Among the objects were the Llano Quemado altar screen, a hide painting, bultos, retablos, textiles, tinwork, tools and utensils, engravings, architectural woodwork, horse gear, weapons, jewelry, straw work, an ex-voto, a rawhide violin, and contemporary wood carvings. Throughout ensuing years, as both Museum of New Mexico and society curator, E. Boyd continued efforts to acquire pieces of traditional Hispanic material culture for both collections. She traveled extensively, usually in a yellow pickup truck she called "Canary," cultivating friendships with many people throughout the state.[7] Individuals began to seek her out to donate or sell objects to the collection. Local collectors and Hispanic families, many of whom owned objects that had been handed down for generations, began to make generous donations. In the mid-1950s Alan C. Vedder approached E. Boyd for advice on the restoration of a retablo he had recently purchased from a local dealer.[8] The retablo was framed by a raised molding with a portion missing. Boyd, who disliked carving wood herself, suggested that Vedder carve a replacement piece that she might then paint and attach to the frame. When Vedder returned with the carved molding Boyd was so impressed by his handiwork that she suggested he carve other pieces for her restoration efforts on bultos and retablos in the society and museum collections. Thus began a working relationship that would last the remainder of their lives. Boyd and Vedder restored thousands of objects in the Spanish Colonial Arts Society and the Museum of New Mexico collections, as well as pieces in private collections and churches.[9] These two individuals, both strong-willed characters, were selfless in their dedication to the collection and to the restoration and preservation of its objects, many of which would otherwise have been lost. They worked diligently to acquire pieces for the society's collection. The two also took objects that had been almost destroyed and with great care and patience restored them using conservation techniques E. Boyd had developed in the early 1950s for artifacts unique to New Mexico. As early as the 1930s the society had acquired pieces imported to New Mexico during the colonial period and the nineteenth century, including Mexican blankets, shawls, and painted chests. Boyd expanded this aspect of the collection by consciously seeking comparative items from Latin America and Spain that could have been imported to New Mexico and might therefore have served as prototypes for traditional New Mexican objects. This policy encouraged gifts from numerous donors who had traveled and collected in Spain or Latin America; such donations included South American silver given by Mrs. Henry Lyman and women's ornamental hair combs given by Mrs. Cornelia G. Thompson. Alan and Ann Vedder made two trips to Spain in the early 1960s to collect objects similar to New Mexican traditional artwork or similar to objects known to have been imported to New Mexico.[10] Prior to these trips Alan discussed in great detail with E. Boyd the different types of material he and Ann should search for in Spain. They purchased provincial religious paintings and sculptures to compare with New Mexican bultos and retablos, as well as Spanish majolica ceramics, metal tools, and utensils similar to fragments excavated from colonial archaeological sites in New Mexico. The Vedders purchased in Spain a total of thirty-one objects for the society's collection. **I**n 1962 Mr. and Mrs. John Gaw Meem donated an extremely important collection of New Mexican textiles to the society. Acquired by the Meems in 1939, it had been compiled by the knowledgeable amateur archaeologist Harry P. Mera, with the assistance of Santa Fe dealer James MacMillan, for the purpose of illustrating the range and development of the Spanish weaving tradition in New Mexico.[11] This collection of thirty-four textiles, among them Rio Grande blankets and two *jergas,* reflected the variety of design elements, weaving techniques, dye selection, and influences from Mexican and later American commercial imports. Still considered one of the most select and comprehensive collections of New Mexican textiles, the Mera collection is often consulted by scholars and weavers. **I**n 1952 the reactivated society adopted a resolution to "undertake to furnish and install the contents of an old New Mexican house and outbuildings from the Spanish Colonial collections [of the society]."[12] Although it was agreed in early 1953 to postpone these particular plans, the desire to encourage and participate in contextual exhibitions depicting Hispanic life in New Mexico persisted in the society's projects. In the 1950s and 1960s, E. Boyd helped install several Spanish Colonial exhibitions and period rooms in the Palace of the Governors, including a re-creation of a northern New Mexico chapel and a Mexican period room.[13] The two displays included objects on loan from the Spanish Colonial Arts Society, and both rooms are still on display at the Palace of the Governors. When the living museum El Rancho de las Golondrinas opened at La Cienega in 1972, it displayed some twenty objects from the society's collection. Many are still there, including doors, windows, shutters, furniture, utensils, crosses, bultos, a loom, and an altar. **D**uring the early 1960s, in an effort to extend awareness of Hispanic culture beyond the region, both Alan Vedder and E. Boyd participated in the installation of long-term exhibitions of Spanish colonial New Mexican material outside New Mexico. Vedder's 1961 installation of an exhibition of two-and-a-half New Mexican period rooms in the American Museum at Bath, England, is still on view. In 1963 Boyd supervised installation of an eighteenth-century New Mexican period room at the Smithsonian Institution in Washington, D.C. **W**ith the death of E. Boyd in 1974, the Spanish Colonial Arts Society lost probably the most influential member in its history. Having worked at Boyd's side for twenty years, Alan Vedder, accompanied by his wife, Ann, was fully prepared to carry on Boyd's work. He began by receiving and processing the many artifactual and monetary donations made in memory of E. Boyd. Some of the funds contributed

were used to purchase objects for the collection; others were applied toward the 1983 publication edited by Marta Weigle with Claudia Larcombe and Samuel Larcombe, *Hispanic Arts and Ethnohistory: New Papers Inspired by the Work of E. Boyd*. **T**hrough the years E. Boyd and the Vedders arranged various substantial bequests benefitting the society, including significant gifts by Norma Fiske Day, Eleanor Bedell, H. M. Berg, Jr., Margretta Dietrich, Cady Wells, and eventually the Vedders themselves. Other major gifts came from Kenneth M. Chapman, Lois Field, Ina Sizer Cassidy, Byron Harvey III, Rebecca S. James, Frank E. Mera, Cornelia G. Thompson, and Amelia Elizabeth White, among others. Mr. and Mrs. John Gaw Meem made a significant gift

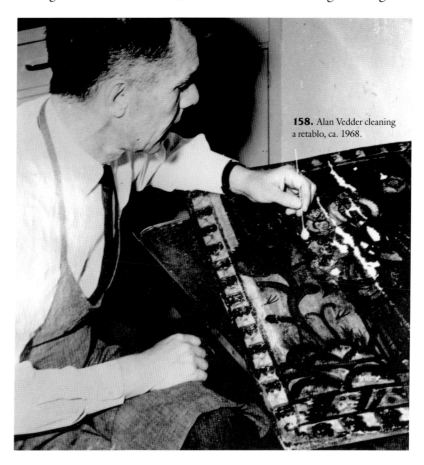

158. Alan Vedder cleaning a retablo, ca. 1968.

of more than one hundred bultos and retablos in 1985. All have greatly enriched the society's collection. **T**he bulk of the Spanish Colonial Arts Society collection is housed and cared for at the Museum of New Mexico's Museum of International Folk Art in Santa Fe. All acquisition decisions, however, are made by the society's Collection Committee. New acquisitions are processed by the society's curator together with the museum's curators and turned over to the Museum of International Folk Art as per the original loan agreement. In 1979 society curator Alan Vedder and the museum staff undertook an inventory of the society's collection. **A** second inventory was begun in 1988, after William Field, Ann Vedder, and Alan Vedder conceived the idea of publishing

159. Crucifix by anonymous artist, ca. 1850. Spanish Colonial Arts Society Collection, on loan to El Rancho de las Golondrinas Museum.

a book that would show the public the essential, largely undisplayed collection and serve as "our museum on paper." At that time Alan Vedder started to reinventory and redocument the collection with the assistance of society board member Donna Pierce. After carefully reading through the accession records and making notes of any questions, abbreviations, discrepancies, or unclear comments, Pierce began a series of taped interviews with both Vedders in late 1988. Proceeding chronologically through the accession records, they discussed in detail the collection, conservation, and exhibition history of many pieces. Ten, ninety-minute interviews were taped, most with Alan Vedder following Ann's death in late January 1989. Vedder, Pierce, and museum curator Robin Farwell Gavin then commenced a hands-on inventory of the collection in October 1989. Each piece was photographed and each photograph numbered and labeled with significant information for use in the research, writing, and design of this book. Pierce assumed the position of society curator and continued the photo-documentation inventory after Alan's death in December. With able and generous assistance from society volunteer and board member Sandra Osterman, by 1992 the bulk of the collection had been processed. Upon the death of Ann Vedder in January 1989, Alan intensified his efforts towards the book in her memory. When Alan Vedder died in December 1989, the society continued the project in their honor. The Vedders left their private collection of some five hundred pieces of Hispanic art and material culture to the society. Pierce and Gavin processed this collection, and in July 1991 Gavin curated an exhibition entitled "Masterworks from the Vedder Collection" at the Changing Gallery in the Hispanic Heritage Wing of the Museum of International Folk Art.

The Hispanic Heritage Wing's long-term inaugural exhibition, "Familia y Fé/Family and Faith," had opened in July 1989 before Alan Vedder's death. It includes approximately seventy objects from the society's collection. Another sixty-three pieces from the society's collection are now on long-term display in the Palace of the Governors in two major exhibits about Spanish life that opened in 1992: "Another Mexico: Spanish Life on the Upper Rio Grande" and "Society Defined: The Hispanic Resident of New Mexico in 1790." Both continue the long tradition of cooperation between the society and the "old Palace."

Unique in its range of focus from the religious to the mundane in arts and material culture, the Spanish Colonial Arts Society collection also attempts to place the traditional art and culture of New Mexico in the context of the rest of the Hispanic world. It includes objects from Spain, Latin America, the Caribbean, the Philippines, and even Goa, the former Portuguese colony off the west coast of India. Comparative religious imagery, particularly of saints, comes from Italy, Russia, Greece, and Romania. There are also comparative examples that may have been imported to New Mexico from New England or from other countries, especially China. As part of the society's goal to encourage the continuation of traditional art in New Mexico, the collection also includes numerous twentieth-century objects, both by Revival-period

98

and contemporary artists. Within this latter category special attention has been paid to collecting pieces inspired by historic objects in the society's or museums' collections. The historical, contemporary, and comparative themes combine to produce a collection with admirable breadth in its inclusion of pieces from all over the Hispanic Catholic world and with true depth in its incorporation of objects from all aspects of life in Hispanic New Mexico of yesterday and today.

NOTES

1. Unless otherwise noted, documentation for this chapter is in Marta Weigle, "The First Twenty-Five Years of the Spanish Colonial Arts Society," and Ann Vedder, "History of the Spanish Colonial Arts Society, Inc., 1951–1981," in Weigle with Claudia Larcombe and Samuel Larcombe, eds., *Hispanic Arts and Ethnohistory in the Southwest: New Papers Inspired by the Work of E. Boyd* (Santa Fe: Ancient City Press; Albuquerque: University of New Mexico Press, 1983), 181–217. Copies of unpublished Spanish Colonial Arts Society accession records (hereafter SCAS) are maintained by the Society curator and the Museum of International Folk Art, Museum of New Mexico (hereafter MNM), Santa Fe.

2. SCAS L.5.28-1.

3. SCAS L.5.28-1 through L.5.53-26.

4. Unpublished files, Palace of the Governors, MNM. Some of these forty-eight pieces may have been lent by Society members since only thirty-five appear in the accession records compiled in the 1950s.

5. SCAS L.5.52-1 through L.5.52-52. Donors in 1952 included Eleanor Brownell and Alice Howland, Ina Sizer Cassidy, Elmer Shupe, María Salazar, Cornelia G. Thompson, Mary Cabot Wheelwright, and Amelia Elizabeth White.

6. SCAS L.5.28-1 through L.5.54-85, esp. L.5.53-21, L.5.53-26, L.5.54-85ff; Marjorie F. Lambert, personal communication, January 1994; Alan C. Vedder, personal communication, 2 March 1989. Although the objects were used in Palace of the Governors exhibitions and under the care of a Palace curator, because of space considerations many were stored in the basement of the MNM's Fine Arts Museum.

7. Alan C. Vedder, personal communication, 6 April 1989.

8. Alan C. Vedder, personal communication, 2 October 1989.

9. Detailed descriptions of their conservation work are in unpublished SCAS and MNM accession records. Also see E. Boyd, "Señor Santiago de Chimayó," *El Palacio* 63, 3 (March 1956): 69-72; E. Boyd, "The Conservation of New Mexican Santos and Other Painted and Gessoed Objects," *El Palacio* 74, 4 (Winter 1967): 19-34; Boyd, *Popular Arts of Spanish New Mexico* (Santa Fe: Museum of New Mexico Press, 1974). For a discussion of conservation techniques see Keith Bakker, "Aesthetic and Cultural Considerations for the Conservation of Hispanic New Mexican Religious Art" (M.A. thesis, Antioch University, 1994).

10. Alan and Ann Vedder, personal communications, 10, 17, 18 January 1989; Alan Vedder, personal communication, 6 April 1989. Specific acquisitions made in Spain and the justification for them are discussed in unpublished SCAS and MNM accession records for 1962.

11. H. P. Mera, *Spanish-American Blanketry,* with an introduction by Kate Peck Kent (Santa Fe: School of American Research, 1987).

12. Vedder, "History," 206.

13. E. Boyd, "Recently Installed Exhibits of the Spanish Colonial Arts Department in the Palace of the Governors," *El Palacio* 62, 3 (March 1955): 88–90.

Appendix B: The Spanish Colonial Arts Society Collection in the Museum of International Folk Art: Historical Artifacts

The Spanish colonial collection at the Museum of New Mexico's Museum of International Folk Art in Santa Fe includes some six thousand items from the collections of the Museum of New Mexico, the Spanish Colonial Arts Society, the International Folk Art Foundation, the School of American Research, and the Archdiocese of Santa Fe. It focuses on Hispanic folk art of the American Southwest from the eighteenth and nineteenth centuries: religious bultos, retablos, paintings on hide, furniture, tinwork, jewelry, textiles, household utensils, tools, agricultural equipment, horse gear, silver, and architectural elements. Because of its depth, scope, quality, supporting research, and important regional Hispanic focus, the Spanish colonial collection is considered one of the foremost of its type in the United States. Fully one-third of this significant collection belongs to the Spanish Colonial Arts Society and has

ROBIN FARWELL GAVIN

been on long-term loan to the museum since 1952. With the support and collaboration of the society and its curators E. Boyd, Alan Vedder, and Donna Pierce, the museum has been able to make available to researchers and the general public, through exhibits, publications, lectures, and workshops, objects that it would not otherwise have been able to share. The society's collection not only augments and complements the museum's; it contains some of the most important pieces housed there. The society's first catalogued item, a nineteenth-century altar screen by José Rafael Aragón from the church of Our Lady of Carmen in Llano Quemado and on view in the Palace of the Governors, fortunately remains in New Mexico as one of only three altar screens housed in the state's museums. The society has also made significant purchases of bultos, retablos, paintings on hide, metalwork, furniture, textiles, and household and agricultural implements, all of which have helped to shape the collections at the Museum of International Folk Art. The acquisition of the Meem collection in 1985 and the Vedder collection in 1990 brought significant pieces into the state museum and made them accessible to the public for study and exhibition. Some items of particular interest in the society's collection are the retablo that identifies the artist Molleno, a retablo signed by José Rafael Aragón, two bultos of La Muerte (Death) or Doña Sebastiana, one of the few painted chests from New Mexico, and prototypical examples from Spain and Spanish colonies, including a splendid eighteenth-century *estofado* (carved, gilded, and etched) figure of the Archangel Michael. All of these pieces and their supporting background information are

available to researchers. Contemporary artists take advantage of this opportunity by coming to the museum and visiting the collections areas, and studying traditional styles, techniques, and pigments. Many use objects belonging to the Spanish Colonial Arts Society as prototypes and inspiration for their own work. Scholars and researchers also consult the extensive accession records and accompanying documents that have been maintained on the society's collections. Students from grammar through graduate schools often visit the collections, and some return independently to work on individual projects. Since the Museum of International Folk Art opened in 1953, some two hundred exhibits have been installed, seventy-one dealing with Hispanic arts. Objects from the society's collection have enriched many of these exhibitions, especially the thirty-five focused on colonial materials. The first comprehensive exhibit ever featuring the Spanish colonial art of New Mexico, "Popular Arts of Colonial New Mexico," was installed at the museum in 1959. Like exhibits that followed in the next fifteen years, it was curated by E. Boyd, then curator of both the museum's and the society's collections. "Popular Arts of Colonial New Mexico" included several re-created room interiors—a chapel, a *morada,* two bedrooms (pre- and post-1821), two kitchens (Spanish and New Mexican), and a *portal*—as well as displays of other religious and secular items. The exhibit and its accompanying brochure introduced the public to the Spanish colonial art of the Southwest. "Traditional New Mexico Crafts" in 1960 was a smaller exhibit but still showed the range of Spanish New Mexican arts, both religious and secular, from the colonial and Territorial periods. In 1963 three exhibits incorporating pieces from the society's collection opened: "Indigo," "Comparative Santos," and "Río Grande Blankets." "Indigo" displayed seventy-three textiles from around the world dating from pre-Columbian times to the present. The fifty-four images of saints in "Comparative Santos" demonstrated the similarities among depictions of the same saint throughout Spain and its colonies. The H. P. Mera collection of textiles, donated to the Spanish Colonial Arts Society by Mr. and Mrs. John Gaw Meem, was featured in "Río Grande Blankets." Two exhibits in 1964 closely examined the work of the New Mexican santero: "18th Century Santeros of New Mexico" and "New Mexico Santos, 1800–1850." In these exhibits E. Boyd introduced her groundbreaking research into the identification of artists and styles in New Mexican folk art. These exhibits were followed in 1969 by Boyd's popular "The New Mexico

Santero," her final, definitive exhibit of the religious art of New Mexico before her death in 1974. Seventy-six of the show's four hundred objects belonged to the society. "Días de Mas, Días de Menos" ("Days of Plenty, Days of Want"), curated by Christine Mather in 1976, explored the daily life of Hispanic New Mexico through material culture. "Spanish Textile Tradition of New Mexico and Colorado" opened in 1978 under the guidance of Nora Fisher. This exhibit and its accompanying publication and workshops highlighted valuable historical information on traditional techniques, styles, and dyes used by weavers today. Both shows included many objects from the society's collection. The ten-year "Baroque to Folk" exhibit that opened in 1978 displayed 150 religious images demonstrating the translation of the prevailing late Spanish baroque style into regional artistic expressions throughout the Spanish colonies and included society pieces from New Mexico and the rest of the Hispanic Catholic world. "Carpinteros and Cabinetmakers: Furniture Making in New Mexico 1600–1900" was the culmination of three years' research by Lonn Taylor and Dessa Bokides. This 1983 exhibit, featuring many society objects and items from private collections, was the first at the museum to take an in-depth look at this craft and the skill and knowledge of the artists. Taylor and Bokides's accompanying brochure and 1987 book, *New Mexican Furniture 1600–1940: The Origins, Survival, and Revival of Furniture Making in the Hispanic Southwest,* remain the primary sources for information about the *carpintero* tradition in New Mexico. The Hispanic Heritage Wing, designed to meet the demand for a permanent exhibit space for the growing historic and contemporary Hispanic collections at the Museum of International Folk Art, opened in 1989. The Spanish Colonial Arts Society was among the many supporters who helped make the wing possible. The inaugural exhibition, "Familia y Fé/ Family and Faith," was realized by guest curator William Wroth with the help of Helen Lucero, the museum's curator of contemporary southwestern Hispanic art. The nearly four hundred objects in this show, some seventy of them from the society's collection, delineate the art of historic New Mexico through the themes of faith and family, two enduring sources of strength and continuity in Hispanic culture. This larger exhibit is expected to be a ten-year installation. It is complemented by a smaller Changing Gallery in the Hispanic Heritage Wing which has a different exhibit every six months. These temporary installations feature the work of contemporary artists working in traditional arts but on occasion showcase the colonial collection as in "Masterworks from the Vedder Collection" with eighty outstanding pieces from Ann and Alan Vedder's bequest to the Spanish Colonial Arts Society. The society's collections have also been made available for loan to other units of the Museum of New Mexico and to museums across the country. In the last five years society items have been on view in Arizona, California, Colorado, Massachusetts, Minnesota, and Washington, D.C. These exhibits and accompanying publications have been enhanced, and indeed made possible, by the Spanish Colonial

Arts Society collection. Having accepted the responsibility for the care of the society's collection, the museum has used it to fulfill its own mandated missions of education and preservation of New Mexico's cultural heritage. Over the years the Museum of International Folk Art, with the support of the Spanish Colonial Arts Society and its collection, has presented to the public a Spanish colonial collection unparalleled in the world.

160. "Popular Arts of Colonial New Mexico" exhibition, Museum of International Folk Art, 1959.
161. "Familia y Fé/Family and Faith" exhibition in the Hispanic Heritage Wing of the Museum of International Folk Art, 1989. **162.** "Masterworks from the Vedder Collection" exhibition in the Changing Gallery in the Hispanic Heritage Wing of the Museum of International Folk Art, 1991.

Appendix C: The Spanish Colonial Arts Society Collection in the Museum of International Folk Art: Contemporary Artifacts

Largely through its associated International Folk Art Foundation, the Museum of New Mexico's Museum of International Folk Art has acquired a sizable collection of contemporary Hispanic folk art. Although relatively small, the Spanish Colonial Arts Society's collection of some two hundred contemporary artifacts provides a welcome breadth and depth to the museum's other contemporary Hispanic collections. Seven traditional kinds of religious and secular artifacts—bultos, retablos, weaving, *colcha* embroidery, furniture, tinwork, and ironwork—represent the bulk of the society's contemporary collection. Although the society has a respectable collection of works produced by artists during the Revival period of the 1920s and 1930s, most contemporary pieces were created within the last thirty years and usually purchased at the annual Spanish Market. Since 1990 religious artifacts so acquired include *Santa Verónica* by Victor Goler, *Saint Dimas* by Luis Tapia, *Doña Sebastiana* by Horacio Valdez, *Noah's Ark* by Marie Romero Cash, and *San Isidro Labrador (Saint Isidore, Farmer)* by Charles Carrillo. Among the recently acquired secular artifacts are a chest by David E. C de Baca, a screen door by Gloria López Córdova, a Vallero star weaving by Irvin L. Trujillo, and a *colcha* embroidery by Monica Sosaya Halford. The society has sponsored professional advancement workshops at the museum. Master santeros Charles Carrillo and Ramón José López taught two-day workshops in 1991 and 1993. The twenty-one santeros and santeras who attended the first workshop and the eighteen who participated in the second learned carving and painting techniques and viewed the museum's extensive collection of santos. A weaving and dyeing workshop led by master weaver Irvin L. Trujillo and museum curator Helen R. Lucero directly benefited nineteen Hispanic weavers and it utilized the museum and society's vast collections of Spanish colonial weavings as teaching examples. These society-sponsored workshops have proved to be excellent settings for learning; future workshops will focus on other traditional artistic media. Over the course of several years the society has acquired artworks by Hispanic children and newly emerging artists. Additional works by these same artists have sometimes been purchased after a span of a few years, thereby creating a collection

HELEN R. LUCERO

that documents the artistic development of some artists. Such is the case with Felix López, from whom the society recently acquired a Saint Francis bulto. When compared with López's Saint Francis acquired by the International Folk Art Foundation some ten years earlier, it shows his remarkable artistic growth over the past decade. Not until the inauguration of the Hispanic Heritage Wing in July 1989 did the Museum of International Folk Art begin systematically to exhibit contemporary Hispanic artifacts, including those from the society's collection. Permanently dedicated to exhibiting Hispanic art, the wing is divided into two sections: a large semipermanent exhibit space, now showing "Familia y Fé/Family and Faith," and a smaller temporary exhibition space known as the Changing Gallery featuring primarily contemporary Hispanic folk art. Fifteen turn-of-the-century and New Deal-era objects from the society's collection are displayed in the "Agents of Change" section of the "Familia y Fé" exhibition, including a bulto depicting the Flight into Egypt by José Dolores López and a tinwork candle sconce by Francisco Sandoval. All exhibitions in the Changing Gallery between July 1989 and December 1993 have included society-owned artifacts:

July–December 1989	Tradición de Orgullo I/Tradition of Pride I
January–June 1990	Tradición de Orgullo II/Tradition of Pride II
July–December 1990	Hojalatería: Tinwork in New Mexico
January–June 1991	Tamarind Invites: Lithographs by New Mexican Santeros
July–December 1991	Masterworks from the Vedder Collection
January–June 1992	San Ysidro Labrador, Patron Saint of Farmers
July–December 1992	18th Century Threads: The History and Conservation of a Gentleman's Suit
January–June 1993	Across Generations: Hispanic Children and Folk Traditions
July–December 1993	Art of the Santera

Attendance at the Museum of International Folk Art has averaged 507,000 visitors annually during the last three years (1990–93). Public programs attract many additional participants. Curators and educators often show artifacts from museum and society collections to those attending demonstrations, classes, workshops, or performances. **A**rtifacts owned by the Spanish Colonial Arts Society are regularly included in traveling educational kits loaned to public schools and to Museum of New Mexico mobile unit exhibitions that tour the state. Many institutions throughout the country borrow objects for their exhibitions. Various society objects, among them a tin box by José María Apodaca and a relief carving by Celso Gallegos, are included in New York's American Craft Museum's 1994–95 "Within Our Shores: Craft Traditions, 1920–1945" exhibit, which will travel to other venues throughout 1996. **P**hotographers, videographers, and other media personnel are regular users of the society and museum collections. "Art of the Santera" is the museum's latest video. Directed by Helen R. Lucero and edited by videographer Tom McCarthy and Robin Farwell Gavin, it was shot in each featured santera's home and at the 1993 Spanish Market. There are interviews with four santeras: Marie Romero Cash, Monica Sosaya Halford, Gloria López Córdova, and Guadalupita Ortiz—all longtime participants in Spanish Market and represented in the society's collection. **O**n occasion society-owned artifacts have been loaned for religious processions. This was the case in 1992 when a Revival-period bulto of the Virgin of Guadalupe was loaned to José Villegas and his *compadres* for a procession on her December twelfth feast day. They carried the image of the Virgin from La Cienega to the St. Francis Cathedral in Santa Fe, a distance of some twenty miles. An image made by the late Lorenzo López has been loaned annually to the Santa Fe community. It is sometimes carried by the maker's grandson, santero Ramón José López, in a San Ysidro (Saint Isidore) procession that originates at Cristo Rey Church and terminates at a small chapel built by the elder López earlier in this century. **T**he Museum of International Folk Art intends to continue showing society-owned artifacts in future exhibitions in the Changing Gallery of the Hispanic Heritage Wing. Art from southern New Mexico, depictions of animals, *colcha* embroidery, and images of the Virgin are but four of the exhibitions currently planned for the next few years. All artifacts in the "Familia y Fé" exhibition in the Hispanic Heritage Wing will be changed at the turn of the century. Pieces from the society's collection will certainly be included in the twenty-first–century exhibit. **W**ith major plans for expansion at the Museum of New Mexico's Palace of the Governors, many more society-owned artifacts will be used in exhibitions there. The multimillion-dollar Hispanic Cultural Center in Albuquerque, scheduled to be fully operational by the year 2000, will include a large museum and studio component. Because the center will not initially have a collection of its own, it will be necessary to borrow artifacts from organizations such as the Spanish Colonial Arts Society. The growing interest in Hispanic culture and the proliferation of museums and cultural centers across the country will further ensure continued demand for loans from the society's collection. **A**s the twenty-first century approaches, the Spanish Colonial Arts

Society will continue to play a very significant role in the preservation and evolution of Hispanic arts. Through summer and winter Spanish markets, the society will further encourage and promote the creation of traditional Hispanic art forms. The society will preserve and share artifacts through exhibitions, and facilitate the documentation of the history of traditional Hispanic life and culture. In all its activities the Spanish Colonial Arts Society enhances the lives of many people—be they artists, museum visitors, tourists, collectors, or researchers.

163. Irvin Trujillo lectures at Weaving Workshop sponsored by Spanish Colonial Arts Society at Museum of International Folk Art, October 1992. **164.** Instructors and participants study historic textiles at Weaving Workshop sponsored by Spanish Colonial Arts Society at Museum of International Folk Art, October 1992.

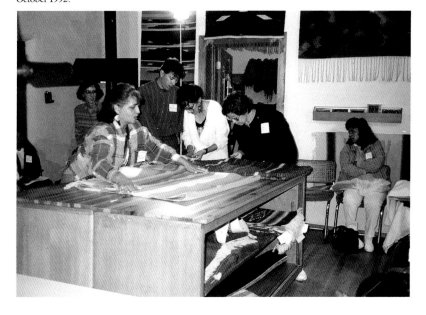

NOTES ON THE CONTRIBUTORS

TERESA ARCHULETA-SAGEL is an expert on the Rio Grande weaving tradition. Her weavings have won numerous awards, have been exhibited internationally, and have been collected by the Museum of International Folk Art, the Heard Museum in Phoenix, the Albuquerque Museum, the Millicent Rogers Museum in Taos, and others. She has taught weaving, consulted on textile research projects, and served as a board member for various cultural institutions.

ROBIN FARWELL GAVIN is Curator of Spanish Colonial Collections at the Museum of New Mexico's Museum of International Folk Art. She is the author of *Traditional Arts of Spanish New Mexico: The Hispanic Heritage Wing at the Museum of International Folk Art* (1994).

HELEN LUCERO was Curator of Southwestern Hispanic Folk Art at the Museum of International Folk Art from 1984 to 1993. In 1995 she became Hispanic Arts Curator at the Fine Arts Museum of the University of New Mexico. She holds a Ph.D. in art education, and her publications include contributions to *Flow of the River/Corre El Río* (1988), *Cuando Hablan Los Santos: Contemporary Santero Traditions from Northern New Mexico* (1995), and *Chimayó Weaving: The Transformation of a Tradition* (in press).

REY MÓNTEZ owns three art galleries in Santa Fe and is a painter, sculptor, and writer. Trained as a lawyer, he resumed a career in the arts in 1987 while living in Spain and researching a novel about early European explorers.

F. CHRISTOPHER OLIVERA is a writer and publicist currently working with the federal government in Santa Fe and Los Alamos. A regular magazine contributor of articles on architecture and design, he has written *Camposantos: The Blessed Fields of New Mexico* (in press).

CARMELLA PADILLA is a freelance writer based in Santa Fe who has written extensively about Hispanic art and culture of New Mexico. Her work has been widely published in newspapers and magazines nationwide, including the *Wall Street Journal, Dallas Morning News,* and *Hispanic, Latina,* and *New Mexico* magazines. Her book, *The Chile Chronicles: Tales of a New Mexico Harvest,* with photographs by Jack Parsons, is scheduled to be published by the Museum of New Mexico Press in 1997.

JACK PARSONS is a photographer who lives in Santa Fe. He has photographed a number of books, among them *Santa Fe and Northern New Mexico* (1991), *Straight from the Heart: Portraits of Traditional Hispanic Musicians* (1990), *Santa Fe Style* (1986), *Native America* (1992), and *True West* (1994).

DONNA PIERCE is Curator of the Spanish Colonial Arts Society and Research Associate at the Palace of the Governors. She has served as research consultant with the Metropolitan Museum of Art, the Brooklyn Museum, and the Santa Barbara Museum of Art, among others. Her publications include (with Gabrielle Palmer) *Cambios: The Spirit of Transformation in Spanish Colonial Art* (1992) and *New World Saints* (1995) and contributions to *Mexican Churches* (1987), *The American Craftsman and the European Tradition* (1989), *Mexican Celebrations* (1990), *Mexico: Splendors of Thirty Centuries* (1990), *Santiago: Saint of Two Worlds* (1991), and *Converging Cultures* (1996).

ANITA GONZALES THOMAS is a retired Santa Fe schoolteacher who has long been active in many aspects of cultural preservation, including the Spanish Colonial Arts Society, La Sociedad Folklórica, the International Folk Art Foundation, and the Colonial New Mexico Historical Foundation. She contributed to Richard B. Stark's *Music of the "Bailes" in New Mexico* (1978). A pioneer in bilingual education, she is a frequent lecturer and consultant on Hispanic culture and received the 1994 Excellence in the Humanities Award from the New Mexico Endowment for the Humanities.

MARTA WEIGLE is University Regents Professor and Chair of the Department of Anthropology at the University of New Mexico. Her books include *Brothers of Light, Brothers of Blood: The Penitentes of the Southwest* (1976), (with Kyle Fiore) *Santa Fe and Taos: The Writer's Era, 1916–1941* (1982), and (with Peter White) *The Lore of New Mexico* (1988). Among her edited volumes are *Hispanic Villages of Northern New Mexico* (1975), (with Lorin W. Brown and Charles L. Briggs) *Hispano Folklife of New Mexico* (1978), (with Claudia Larcombe and Samuel Larcombe) *Hispanic Arts and Ethnohistory in the Southwest* (1983), *Two Guadalupes: Hispanic Legends and Magic Tales from Northern New Mexico* (1987), and (with Barbara A. Babcock) *The Great Southwest of the Fred Harvey Company and the Santa Fe Railway* (1996).

Photo Credits and Accession Numbers

CHAPTER 1:
Fig. 1-Private Collection.
Fig. 2-Photo by Jesse L. Nusbaum,
Museum of New Mexico, neg. no. 61539.
Fig. 3-Photo by Jesse L. Nusbaum,
Museum of New Mexico, neg. no. 13078.
Fig. 4-Photo by Jesse L. Nusbaum,
Museum of New Mexico, neg. no. 10541.
Fig. 5-Photo by Jesse L. Nusbaum,
Museum of New Mexico, neg. no. 61496.
Fig. 6-Museum of New Mexico, neg. no. 75769.
Fig. 7-Museum of New Mexico, neg. no. 40698.
Fig. 8-Museum of New Mexico, neg. no. 60264.
Fig. 9-Museum of New Mexico, neg. no. 11001.
Fig. 10-Museum of New Mexico, neg. no. 117869.
Fig. 11-Museum of New Mexico, neg. no. 66540.
Fig. 12-Museum of New Mexico, neg. no. 46643.
Fig. 13-Museum of New Mexico, neg. no. 14575.
Fig. 14-Photo by L. C. McClure,
Museum of New Mexico, neg. no. 106862.
Fig. 15-Photo by T. Harmon Parkhurst,
Museum of New Mexico, neg. no. 10695.
Fig. 16-Photo by Jesse L. Nusbaum,
Museum of New Mexico, neg. no. 61669.
Fig. 17-Photo by Jesse L. Nusbaum,
Museum of New Mexico, neg. no. 61673.
Fig. 18-Museum of New Mexico, neg. no. 56203.
Fig. 19-Photo by T. Harmon Parkhurst,
Museum of New Mexico, neg. no. 23098.
Fig. 20-Photo by Edward Kemp,
Museum of New Mexico, neg. no. 53578.
Fig. 21-Museum of New Mexico, neg. no. 40288.
Fig. 22-Courtesy History Library,
Palace of the Governors, Museum of New Mexico.
Fig. 23-Private Collection.
Fig. 24-Courtesy El Rancho de Las Golondrinas Museum.
Fig. 25-Papers of the Spanish Colonial Arts Society,
New Mexico State Records Center and Archives.
Fig. 26-Museum of New Mexico, neg. no. 9919.
Fig. 27-Photo by T. Harmon Parkhurst,
Museum of New Mexico, neg. no. 53577.
Fig. 28-Photo by T. Harmon Parkhurst,
Courtesy El Rancho de Las Golondrinas Museum.
Fig. 29-Photo by T. Harmon Parkhurst,
Courtesy El Rancho de Las Golondrinas Museum.
Fig. 30-Photo by Russell Lee, Farm Security Administration
Collection, Library of Congress, LC-USF 34-34264-D.
Fig. 31-Photo by John Collier, Jr., Farm Security Administration
Collection, Library of Congress, LC-USW 3-13762-C.
Fig. 32-Photo by John Collier, Jr., Farm Security Administration
Collection, Library of Congress, LC-USW 3-15218-C.
Fig. 33-Photo by John Collier, Jr., Farm Security Administration
Collection, Library of Congress, LC-USW 3-17872-C.
Fig. 34-Spanish Colonial Arts Society Collection.
Fig. 35-Spanish Colonial Arts Society Collection.
Fig. 36-Spanish Colonial Arts Society Collection.
Fig. 37-Photo by Harold D. Walter,
Museum of New Mexico, neg. no. 58036.
Fig. 38-Photo by Harold D. Walter,
Museum of New Mexico, neg. no. 135147.

CHAPTER 2:
Fig. 39-Spanish Colonial Arts Society Collection.
Fig. 40-Photo by Carol Stryker,
Museum of New Mexico, neg. no. 14248.
Fig. 41-New Mexico State Records Center and Archives.
Fig. 42-Photo by Mack Photo Service, Private Collection.
Fig. 43-Courtesy Mr. and Mrs. William Field.
Fig. 44-Spanish Colonial Arts Society Collection.
Fig. 45-Photo by Tyler Dingee,
Museum of New Mexico, neg. no. 20749.
Fig. 46-Museum of New Mexico, neg. no. 41698.
Fig. 47-Photo by Nancy Hunter Warren.
Fig. 48-Spanish Colonial Arts Society Collection.
Fig. 49-Museum of New Mexico, neg. no. 49289.

CHAPTER 3:
Photo of Celso Gallegos (p. 36) by Ina Sizer Cassidy, ca. 1930,
Museum of New Mexico, neg. no. 9891.
Fig. 50-Spanish Colonial Arts Society Collection accession
numbers L.5.75-5 through 7.
Fig. 51-L.5.90-184. Fig. 52-L.5.55-5.
Fig. 53-L.5.55-3. Fig. 54-L.5.68-18.
Fig. 55-L.5.85-77.
Fig. 56-L.5.80-2. Photo of José Dolores López (p. 38) by
T. Harmon Parkhurst, ca. 1935,
Museum of New Mexico, neg. no. 94470.
Fig. 57-L.5.52-46. Fig. 58-L.5.62-3.
Fig. 59-V.61.7-F. Fig. 60-L.5.59-27.
Fig. 61-L.5.95-21. Fig. 62-L.5.52-45.
Fig. 63-L.5.70-18. Photo of George López (p. 41) by
Emmett P. Haddon, January, 1958,
Museum of New Mexico, neg. no. 151996.
Fig. 64-L.5.52-12. Fig. 65-L.5.79-7.
Fig. 66-L.5.61-89. Fig. 67-L.5.90-69.
Fig. 68-L.5.75-71. Fig. 69-L.5.72-31.
Fig. 70-L.5.90-65.
Fig. 71-L.5.90-64. Photo of Patrocinio Barela (p. 43),
Museum of New Mexico, neg. no. 90196. Photo of Juan Sanchez
(p. 43), Museum of New Mexico, neg. no. 90199.
Fig. 72-L.5.79-6. Fig. 73-V.65.1-B.
Fig. 74-L.5.71-16. Fig. 75-L.5.68-21.
Fig. 76-L.6.77-4. Fig. 77-no V number.
Fig. 78-no V number. Fig. 79-no V number.
Fig. 80-no V number. Fig. 81-no V number.
Fig. 82-no V number. Fig. 83-no V number.
Fig. 84-L.5.54-40. Fig. 85-L.5.69-3.
Fig. 86-L.5.60-2. Fig. 87-L.5.54-7.

CHAPTER 4:
Fig. 88-V.81.1-S.
Fig. 89-L.5.79-11. Photo of Francisco Delgado (p. 50) by
T. Harmon Parkhurst, ca. 1935,
Museum of New Mexico, neg. no. 71180.
Fig. 90-L.5.55-38. Fig. 91-no V number.
Fig. 92-V.65.2-T. Fig. 93-V.58.1-T.

CHAPTER 5:
Color photographs by Jack Parsons; black-and-white
photographs by Nancy Hunter Warren.

CHAPTER 6:
Photographic portraits by Jack Parsons.
Fig. 94-L.5.78-1. Fig. 95-L.5.93-7.
Fig. 96-L.5.92-4. Fig. 97-L.5.91-1.
Fig. 98-L.5.91-3. Fig. 99-L.5.82-2.
Fig. 100-L.5.76-19. Fig. 101-L.5.92-5.
Fig. 102-L.5.93-3. Fig. 103-L.5.92-3.
Fig. 104-L.5.88-1. Fig. 105-L.5.94-12.
Fig. 106-L.5.75-139. Fig. 107-V.82.2-S.
Fig. 108-L.5.86-5. Fig. 109-L.5.88-4.
Fig. 110-L.5.74-12. Fig. 111-L.5.75-70.
Fig. 112-L.5.93-1. Fig. 113-L.5.92-6.
Fig. 114-L.5.92-2. Fig. 115-L.5.94-9.
Fig. 116-L.5.94-20. Fig. 117-L.5.93-2.
Fig. 118-L.5.95-6. Fig. 119-L.5.94-3.
Fig. 120-L.5.94-14. Fig. 121-L.5.94-5.
Fig. 122-L.5.86-4. Fig. 123-L.5.80-3.
Fig. 124-L.5.85-6. Fig. 125-L.5.77-9.
Fig. 126-no V number. Fig. 127-L.5.86-3.
Fig. 128-L.5.81-2. Fig. 129-L.5.75-72.
Fig. 130-L.5.93-10. Fig. 131-L.5.95-2.
Fig. 132-L.5.94-1. Fig. 133-L.5.94-4.
Fig. 134-L.5.93-9. Fig. 135-L.5.77-7.
Fig. 136-L.5.86-2. Fig. 137-L.5.88-5.
Fig. 138-L.5.90-1. Fig. 139-L.5.94-6.
Fig. 140-L.5.91-2. Fig. 141-L.5.92-1.
Fig. 142-L.5.95-5. Fig. 143-L.5.78-2.
Fig. 144-L.5.94-8. Fig. 145-L.5.77-11.
Fig. 146-L.5.94-16. Fig. 147-L.5.79-12.
Fig. 148-L.5.94-7. Fig. 149-L.5.95-3.
Fig. 150-L.5.93-8. Fig. 151-L.5.68-33.
Fig. 152-L.5.77-6. Fig. 153-L.5.85-5.
Fig. 154-L.5.93-5. Fig. 155-no V number.

APPENDICES:
Fig. 156-Photo by Charles Herbert, Museum of New Mexico,
neg. no. 15368.
Fig. 157-Courtesy El Rancho de Las Golondrinas Museum.
Fig. 158-Museum of New Mexico, neg. no. 50016.
Fig. 159-L.5.68-17. Fig. 160-Photo by Laura Gilpin.
Fig. 161-Photo by Blair Clark.
Fig. 162-Photo by Blair Clark.
Fig. 163-Courtesy of Helen Lucero.
Fig. 164-Courtesy of Helen Lucero.

INDEX

Boldface refers to figure numbers.

Patrocinio Barela Donors ($25-$99)

Richard E. Ahlborn
Anonymous in memory of E. Boyd
Charlotte Appella
Mr. and Mrs. Lester Buchanan
Richard and Debby Casillas
Charlene Cerny
Eladio F. and Elna Chavez
Katherine Z. Chiba
Susan Anneke Chittim
Mrs. Frank J. Claffey
Sam and Becky Cordova
Edmund P. Cranz
Mrs. W.P. Cranz
Mr. and Mrs. Ingersoll Cunningham
Anna Belle Day
Volker and Josette de la Harpe
Irene Brandtner de Martinez
Stephanie and David Duff
Mr. and Mrs. Edmond Freeman
Virginia Fryer
Robin Farwell Gavin
Mrs. Alexander Girard
Jack and Elizabeth Graves
Stacey K. or Phyllis L. Gray
Ezell Hammer
Mr. and Mrs. Michael Harris
Mr. and Mrs. George B. Healy
Historic Santa Fe Foundation
Dirk Houtman
Dr. Myra Ellen Jenkins
Jean M. and Anita Romero Jones
Courtney R. Jones
E. Donald and Dr. Janet B. Kaye
Elizabeth Y. Kingman
Kit Carson Historic Museums
Robert and Carol Kurth
Ronald R. Levert
Mr. and Mrs. Owen M. Lopez
Maria Padilla and Jose Floyd Lucero
Mr. and Mrs. Richard Martinez
Mr. and Mrs. James C. Meem
Sharon and Tony Mitchell
Richard and Teresa Montoya and Family
Mr. and Mrs. Simon Mostert
Elizabeth S. Munson
Museum of International Folk Art Staff
Anne Bateman Noss
John and Mary Lou Paxton
Jim and Pat Price

E. Catherine Rayne
Bud and Lois Redding
Mr. and Mrs. George H. Redding, Jr.
Barbe Awalt and Paul Rhetts
Fred Romero
Benjamin N. Saiz
John and Rosemary Samuel
Katherine V. Sayre
Judy and Dick Sellars
Richard E. and Arlene Cisneros Sena
Ms. Martha Sewell
Mimi and Charmaine Sloane
Lynne and Richard Spivey
Mr. and Mrs. Eric Springsted
Consuelo Tedin de Chozas
Dr. and Mrs. J. Robert Thompson
Mr. Stephen E. Watkins
Charles H. and Mary R. Winberg
Gordon and Margaret M. Winkler
Letta and Keith Wofford
Mr. and Mrs. Robert P. Worcester
Jake and Donna Romero Wright

Celso Gallegos Donors ($100-$249)

Grace Vogel Aldworth
Charmay B. Allred
A. Gary Ames
Mr. Samuel B. Ballen
   Ballen and Company
Mrs. Elspeth G. Bobbs
Mr. William Cabrera
Mr. and Mrs. Omer Claiborne
   Claiborne Gallery
Adele H. Cornelius
Maureen Field
Mr. and Mrs. Justin Mark Day
Louisa Garcia-Byrd
Victor Goler
Mr. and Mrs. Wm. M. Hallett
Julius P. Hammer
Mr. and Mrs. Julius Heldman
Susan Cable Herter
Isabel Kuziel
John B. Levert
Felix and Louise Lopez
Rosina Lopez de Short
Maryann McCaffery
Susan McGreevy
Luis Morales
Old World Hardware

Tony D. and Pita H. Ortiz
Dr. Armin Rembe
Edward C. Roe
James H. Russell Agency
Joseph A. Sommer
Lynn Steuer
Malcolm and Rosemarie Stewart
The American Folk Art Society
Anita Gonzales Thomas
Mrs. Sallie Wagner
Marjorie H. Watkins
Mary D. Weigle

The Society would like to express their appreciation to the sponsors of this book

Jose Benito Ortega Donors ($250-$499)

Dr. and Mrs. Julio C. Davila
Mrs. E. B. Healy
Dr. and Mrs. George A. Holloway, Jr.
James and Frances Lieu and the CBS
   Foundation Inc. Matching Grant Program
Marian Love and Betty Bauer
   The Santa Fean Magazine
Owings-Dewey Fine Art
Ray Wolf and Michael Nedbalek
Alithea Olson
Patsey R. Pierce and Carla Pierce

Molleno Donors ($500-$999)

Mr. and Mrs. Georges H. Dapples
George G. Frelinghuysen
Dr. Gregory A. Gordon
Mr. and Mrs. Booker Kelly
Gerald and Kathleen Peters Family Fund
Nancy Thompson Taylor

Jose Rafael Aragon Donors ($1000-$2499)

Anonymous Donation
William N. and Julia L. Ashbey
Bruce B. Donnell
Virginia B. Goodwin
Mr. and Mrs. Hugh Hallgren
International Folk Art Foundation
Don Jacob and Lila A. Madtson
Adele Levi Rand
The New Mexico Arts Division
John and Nancy Meem Wirth